THE VOICE: A MISSIONARY'S CALL TO GIVE HER LIFE

**Dorothy Chapon Kazel
&
Sr. Mary Ann Flannery, S.C.**

PRESS

Dorothy Chapon Kazel
&
Sr. Mary Ann Flannery, S.C.

DEDICATION

All missionaries who lost their lives in El Salvador
and Salvadoran people who suffered and died
with them.

Sr. Diane Pinchot, OSU

ACKNOWLEDGMENTS

R obert White, Former Ambassador to El Salvador; Sr. Collette Livingston, Archivist for the Ursuline Sisters of Cleveland, Ohio; Sr. Kathleen Cooney, OSU, Ursuline College; Sr. Martha Owen, OSU of Cleveland, Ohio: Jill Sberna and Samantha Reefer of John Carroll University, Department of Communication and Theatre Arts; Sr. Anita Maroun, SC; Isabel Blaha, cover artist and, of course, James Kazel, supporter and husband of Dorothy Chapon Kazel and brother of Sr. Dorothy Kazel, OSU.

TABLE OF CONTENTS

FOREWORD

Robert White, Former American Ambassador
to El Salvador

S ister Dorothy Kazel's life spoke to the power of love in the face of fear. Her collected letters tell the story of her gradual awakening to the terrible reality of Central America. These letters testify to Dorothy's growth in faith through her dedication to the people of El Salvador.

Dorothy's smile revealed her joy in working among the poor of Central America. Because she saw the Christ in there people, she did not take to dwell on her own suffering. Her words reflect gratitude for the opportunity to fulfill her vocation by serving the victims of oppression.

The missionary women with whom Dorothy lived, worked and died were intelligent, educated Americans who wanted to be proud of their country. They held strong views on Washington's policies in the region. Drawing on her dialing life experiences, Sister Dorothy begged for an end to United States military assistance to El Salvador because she knew it was contributing to the misery of the common people. I shared Dorothy's concerns, and during my tenure as ambassador, no lethal military assistance reached the Salvadoran security forces.

Salvadoran security forces tortured and killed Sisters Dorothy Kazel, Ita Ford, Maura Clarke, and Miss Jean Donovan near the remote hamlet of San Juan Nonualco. With this barbaric act, the Salvadoran military sent an unambiguous message: We will kill anyone who gets in our way and we are accountable for no one.

After witnessing the disinterment of the bodies of the four women martyrs, I sent a telegram to the US State Department reporting that the women had been executed at point blank range, a standard mark of a Salvadoran military operation. President Carter immediately went on national television and announced that the United States Government would hold the Salvadoran military accountable. He announced that he was suspending military and economic aid to El Salvador until that government demonstrated its resolve to bring the killers to justice.

President Reagan took office in January 20th, 1981, less than three months after the deaths of the four women. Outrage was in short supply in the new administration. When I suggested that the new Secretary of State Alexander Haig condemn the murders, the reply came back that the Salvadoran junta was a government under siege and he was not going to add to its troubles.

Ambassador Jeane Kirkpatrick and Secretary of State Alexander Haig took charge of attacking the reputations of Dorothy, Ita, Maura and Jean, and finding excuses for the Salvadoran military. Kirkpatrick said the nuns were not just nuns but political activists. Haig told a congressional group that the women may have been shot by the military as they tried to run a roadblock. Both statements were untrue and their authors knew them to be untrue.

The new administration, desperate to send massive military assistance to El Salvador, looked for a way to circumvent President Carter's insistence on justice and accountability. They needed someone with credibility to front for them.

Secretary Haig ordered me to send a message from the embassy stating that the Salvadoran government was making a serious effort to solve the crimes and that their investigations were making progress. I refused. Instead, I sent a telegram that stated: "It's amazing to me that the Department can state publicly that the investigation of the nuns' death is proceeding satisfactorily. This is not backed up by any report from the embassy. I reiterate for the record that in my judgment there is no sign of any sincere attempt to locate and punish those responsible for this atrocity."

I knew that my refusal to comply with Haig's order would bring to an end my career as a professional diplomat. Yet I had no choice. It was a matter of both personal ethics and national interest.

The disastrous results of President Reagan's policies should be better known: Never in the history of

Latin America has a country of group of countries suffered such concentrated death and destruction as Central America during the 1980s. Through our proxy armies in El Salvador, Nicaragua and Honduras, more than 150,000 civilians followed Dorothy, Maura, Ita, and Jean to the grave. More than two million terrorized people fled to the United States and entered as illegal immigrants. And it was the American-trained military units, such as the Atlacatl Battalion that compiled the worst human rights records, wiping out entire villages and then denying their responsibility with the help of the US officials.

After twelve years of war, the Salvadoran government and the FMLN revolutionary coalition signed a UN-brokered peace agreement. This accord provided for a truth commission to investigate the conduct of war. The UN report entitled "From Madness to Hope," concludes that almost all important officials concerned "have lied" about who was responsible for the ongoing torture, murder, and repression. The report found that 85 percent of the violence must be attributed to the Salvadoran security forces.

One commentary on the UN Truth Commission report listed the names of ambassadors to El Salvador who "knew the truth but remained silent or covered up the crimes." It is a matter of some pride to me and to my family that my name is not on that list.

The publication of Dorothy's letters will ensure that the spirit of her dedicated courage will live on for generations.

PREFACE

Dorothy Chapon Kazel

I am often asked, "What was Sister Dorothy Kazel like"?

Her life and mine intersected when I married Dorothy's brother, Jim Kazel in 1959. Dorothy was 20 at the time. Neither of us had a sister so we immediately determined we were going to be sisters, not sisters-in-law.

And we were.

Family life with Dorothy was joyful and unpredictable for its frivolity and adventure. Still, she bore a serious side, reflective of a growing spirituality. She grew up in a Lithuanian neighborhood in Cleveland, Ohio, attended the parish school, took piano lessons, roller skating lessons, and excelled in baseball. She was a bubbly, blond, wiry child who grew into a stunning beauty as an adolescent enrolled in Notre Dame Catholic Girls High School.

Later, Dorothy became a student at St. John College of Cleveland that trained teachers for

Cleveland's parochial schools. She had abandoned her original plan of becoming a medical secretary and responded to the urge to do something for others in the context of her faith. Meanwhile, she had accepted an engagement ring and began making wedding plans for the summer of 1960.

To all appearances, she was happily constructing a future based on family and faith.

During her engagement, however, Dorothy began to have doubts about nurturing such a "tidy" future, the manifestation of the American dream. She was teaching at St. Roberts School in Euclid, Ohio and was noticing in the Ursuline Sisters who taught at the school, a peace and generosity of service she found appealing. Years later she confided to me and friends that one evening, while working at St. Roberts, she felt as if her bedroom were suffused in sunlight. She felt a loving pervasive presence of God that suggested she might not be intended for marriage.

A retreat for engaged women at the diocesan retreat house underscored the finality of this decision. Dorothy Kazel entered the Ursuline novitiate in September, 1960.

Her years of training and education as an Ursuline Sister form the period of maturation in her faith and in her call to greater service to the poor. Dorothy had always been attracted to the marginated of society. She felt there was more she could be doing to challenge the injustices which forced many people into lives of desperation. In 1965 she accepted an assignment to teach high school girls and to begin training as a counselor for them. By 1974 she had earned a master's in counseling. She volunteered to teach the Papago Indians one summer in Arizona, an experience that further nurtured her growing attraction to mission life. This was a time of conflicting decisions once again. Here was Sister Dorothy Kazel with an advanced degree in counseling and a heart moving toward a greater commitment to the poor. Her prayer life began challenging her to determine if the Cleveland Diocesan Mission in El Salvador was, in fact, the place where she must serve. In early summer of 1974, Dorothy requested to begin training for El Salvador. A note in her prayer book, dated June 24, 1974 reflects the anguish of her decision and the desire to do God's will:

"Jesus—I am fighting you again

I am fighting " dying to self"

I am fighting "stripping myself of my own willful pleasures"

Jesus—I am sick at the pit of my stomach. Give me the peace to know I am doing your will and the joy that goes with it. Help me overcome my selfish whims and desires.

Jesus—I believe you will do this and handle the whole situation.

Praise and glory to you for being my creator."

From this day on, Sister Dorothy Kazel's life became immersed in the missionary vocation. She found herself in a whirlwind of activities: preparation of native persons as catechists; instruction of women in basic nutrition, food preparation, hygiene, childcare, instruction of children for the sacraments, arranging liturgies and visiting the sick.

Though Dorothy and her colleagues became aware of the worsening political situation in El Salvador they were tirelessly focused on helping their people to survive despite the government's distrust of the Catholic Church which had promoted the teaching of justice for oppressed workers and farmers.

I re-read the writings of my sister-in-law some 25 years after the horrendous fate that awaited her, Sister Maura Clark, Sister Ita Ford, and Jean Donovan on a remote hillside in El Salvador; I get an overwhelming sense of Dorothy's innocence of purpose. I am sure the same is true about the other three women as well. Perhaps it is time to focus on that purpose without the distraction of politics, war, and distrust.

For this reason, we—the editors of this book—have decided to publish the letters of Sister Dorothy Kazel, OSU. These writings demonstrate the 'ordinariness' of this modern martyr. They suggest that all of us, who truly profess a belief in Jesus working within us, will wrestle with doubt, will second guess our choices, will look for assurance for our actions, and will call on our faithful, loving God for direction. The reader will trace a progression in the spiritual life of a woman who moved courageously toward the fulfillment of God's will for her just as the reader must do in his or her life.

Who was Sister Dorothy Kazel?

SR. DOROTHY ANNOUNCES SHE WILL BECOME A MISSIONARY

Dorothy Chapon Kazel

I remember the day Sr. Dorothy told me of her intention to become a missionary to El Salvador. I wrote this essay following that day.

It was a perfect afternoon unwinding in an April breeze. I just finished baking a batch of scones, later to be topped with strawberry jam and whip cream. Suddenly, I heard a knock at my front door. Going toward it I remember wondering who it could be. I shall never forget as I opened the door, smiling face and summer warmth that greeted me. Like an unplanned picnic, Sister Dorothy's surprise visit was a welcome sight.

Inviting her in and welcoming her with open arms, I asked her to partake of afternoon tea and scones. The house was quiet, owing to the fact my youngest child was napping. The scent of bakery filled the dining room as we sat and enjoyed our "English tea."

It was a very special moment when Sister Dorothy mentioned that she was becoming a missionary and would be leaving for El Salvador. I was shocked by the thought that soon she would be leaving Beaumont High School where she taught and counseled students for some unheard of place. "Where in the world is El Salvador?" I blurted out, between sips of tea.

It was as if the reality of her words made it even more real to her. "Yes, Dorothy, I'm going from guidance counselor to missionary." Tears swelled in our eyes as mixed emotions filled our hearts. I remember her saying "You now have another place to visit."

I further recall how moved she was by missionary Alice Brickman's introduction, at mass one morning. Sister Dorothy said, "It made me realize my narrowness and how I have to grow into awareness of the universal brotherhood of man. Maybe that's what El Salvador is all about—expanding my narrow vision."

I sat there pondering how Sister Dorothy was facing a challenging commitment on the other side of the globe and I was handling one within the confines of my home raising my family. How different, yet similar was our goals, for we both shared the belief that life is love and growth.

I will always remember such pleasant memories at teatime in 1974.

**Sr. Dorothy Kazel, OSU and sister-in-law
Mrs. Dorothy Chapon Kazel**

INTRODUCTION

Sr. Mary Ann Flannery, SC

The letters we have selected for this volume are divided into three periods of Sister Dorothy's call to mission. The first period includes her letters as she begins life as a missionary. They are full of excitement in learning about a new culture and language and they describe in detail Dorothy's connecting of family to her new culture. She purchases gifts regularly – and thoughtfully assigns each to this family member or that almost as a way of introducing the family to the culture with which she would now immerse herself.

In these letters, Dorothy, and her friend Sister Martha Owen, OSU, are the new kids on the block: On the Cleveland, Ohio Mission Team in El Salvador. She and Martha joined the team in July 1974. Not long after, they were sent for more language training in Costa Rica and by December 1974, were headed back to El Salvador to begin their ministry.

The two returned to El Salvador in December 1974, and resumed their work in Chirilagua, a very poor village in the north of the country. By April of 1975 both Dorothy and Martha were assigned to the mission of La Union farther north in the country. The goal of the team for this mission was to transfer the American pastoral leadership of the parish to native Salvadoran clergy. Here Dorothy and Martha joined fellow Clevelander, Fr. Jim McCreight, and his two Salvadoran assistants, Fr. Lionel Cruz and Fr. Miguel Ventura. One of Dorothy's letters (August 8, 1975) refers to an anticipated visit from Fr. Ken Meyers of the Cleveland team who was working in Zaragoza, several hours south of La Union. Ken had been trying to secure a living place for Dorothy and Martha in Zaragoza because once the transfer of leadership was complete in La Union; the two nuns were to join Ken in Zaragoza

In the space of two years the new missionaries had served in two large village parishes and had undergone several months of advanced language training. Throughout it all Dorothy remains upbeat. She does not disclose personal apprehensions other than the occasional reference sounding like home-sickness. Meantime, ravaging clouds of political unrest are gathering and though she is aware of this, she believes that her focus on the needs of the people is all that is required of her.

During her years in El Salvador, Dorothy communicated mostly on audiotape sending the tapes with an accompanying brief letter. The tapes became sporadic diaries recorded over several days and often re-used. They were taken back and forth from team members to their families by visitors who came to Salvador at the rate of at least once a month and often more frequently. Many of the tapes are in the archives of the Ursuline Sisters of Cleveland. They are extremely helpful in documenting the developing political situation and the war itself. The tapes are rife with eyewitness accounts of kidnapping and the general unrest of the country. However, the tapes were meant to be shared among the friends and families of the missionaries making the narratives disjointed and full of information not relevant to the history unfolding at this time. It seems to us that the purest documentation of Dorothy's thoughts, lending insights to her spirituality, is in the letters she regularly sent to family and friends.

It is interesting to note that the letters of her first year in El Salvador are dated including the year. Somewhere during 1975, however, the letters do not indicate the year in which they are written. Placing these letters in as accurate a time scheme as possible required considerable sleuthing on the part of the editors. We hope we have done this successfully.

The reader must bear in mind that this volume is a compendium of selected letters though not many were left out. While Dorothy was a faithful correspondent, she was not a voluminous one. Her letters are fairly brief, slowly disclosing over time her mounting concerns about the fate of the people and fellow missionaries.

Religious epistolary rhetoric – content of letters – has long been collected and analyzed beginning with the Epistles of the New Testament to the modern period of history. Scholars ferret through their collections to glean the insights of the writer because such letters were, most often, written for the purpose of analysis. Consider for instance the letters of St. Catherine of Siena urging the exiled Pope Gregory XI to return to Rome from Avigon thus ensuring that the seat of Catholicism would remain an independent seat. Some 400 letters of Catherine are extant having been sent to popes, princes, soldiers, priests, statesmen, etc. on behalf of the Church. Or, note, the famous missives sent by Ignatius of Antioch who wrote to faith communities as he endured his own death march from Antioch to Rome to be consumed by the lions for his defiance against Trojan's belief that idol gods lived and gave inspiration to believers and not the God of Jesus Christ.

By no stretch of the imagination are Sister Dorothy's letters in such a category. It is their very narrative purity, their simplicity, humor, and brevity that captivate the reader. Nonetheless, they are in the category of faith-writing, if you will, forming a narrative of Catholic missionary life in modern times. Dorothy writes as if she is speaking with you. And, if she could speak from beyond, Sister Dorothy would most assuredly question the value of this collection. She would see her writings as meaning-less and, if published at all, why not with those of her fellow martyrs?

The editors have noted, however, that the letters do provide insights to the spiritual growth of a most remarkable woman who dies a martyr's death. They move gracefully from attachment to the faith that provided answers in its simple orthodoxy, to a changed faith which drew Dorothy from the orthodox interpretation to her religion to an openness that challenges the spiritual life to look at all options for growth. Finally, a consummation of all that grew within the soul prompting the choice, a decision, praxis of the spirituality developed thus far.

Theologian Raminondo Panikkar has elegantly articulated these levels of growth so manifested in Sister Dorothy's life. He has written that the first stage of the Christian spiritual life is orthodoxy, when we live our life of faith as it has been organized for us. The rules are clear; the parameters set. There is a joy in following this paradigm – until we learn more about our faith. If a Christian is growing, the comfort of orthodoxy will not last. One realizes there is more to one's faith. There is mystery and the perduring excitement of a Christ manifesting Himself in less tractable, less assuring ways. Panikkar calls this period orthopoesis, or the period in which we "identify our faith with the attitude and moral development" that leads to our destiny. (Panikkar 195). Finally, a Christian who is fervently living his or her vocation and has come through the first two states will enter the final one, orthopraxis, or the consummation of the faith in ultimate union with God. Everything one does, everything one practices, is for God alone.

Sister Dorothy Kazel's life mirrors this template with uncommon synchronicity. The writings we present in this volume are based on these very periods of her spiritual life. In this first section we will read of a Dorothy caught up in the excitement and challenge of preparing for the life of a missionary. In this effervescent woman, our loving God is "stirring up" something. For the time being, though, she is aware of His slow methodical intention of claiming her entirely for Himself. She is tentatively excited over meeting different people, buying gifts, learning her Spanish. She misses her parents and her family but is sure of her plan for this exciting work.

BEGINNING THE SEEDS OF GETTING TO KNOW THE POOR

Sr. Mary Ann Flannery, SC

In November, 1967, Sr. Dorothy Kazel wrote to her superior, Mother Annunciata, O.S.U., expressing her wish to begin training as a missionary. The letter traces Dorothy's history as a young Ursuline Sister and how the Spirit worked in her leading to the request to serve in El Salvador.

Dear Mother:

In a way this deciding whether or not you are qualified for a position can be a very humbling experience. It really makes you stop and take inventory of what you are, what you have, and what you can give to others.

Mother, I have always been of the nature of a person eager to be on the move—-to go to new places, to meet new people, to learn to understand these people, and to help them.

Before I entered I traveled to the West Coast four times; it was then that I was first impressed with the Spanish and Indian people. I wanted to stay, to get to know them, and to help them. I had even "day dreamed" that my parents would disown me and leave me there. Then I entered. As a junior sister I attended Ursuline College. While at the College, I took a course about Latin America and since then I have even more earnestly had the desire to go there. The countries and people hold a special appeal for me. It may sound strange — I am eager to go anywhere — but if we had opened a mission in Africa rather than Latin America, I am sure I would be less inclined to want to go. My preference is Latin America, although as I say, I would be willing to go anywhere.

On Sunday, October 22, I did talk this matter over with my parents. They have given their consent. They were very surprised to hear we were going to open a foreign mission and said they couldn't quite imagine themselves eager to go; but, if this is what I wanted, they would want it too.

In regard to qualifications, Mother, these are what I thought may be of some value:

1. I am presently 28 years old and consider myself as mature as I should be at this time.
2. I have had two years experience in teaching elementary school (third grade, St. Robert Bellarmine School) which I enjoy very much.

3. I have been trained in the "practical arts" of the business field and have had some experience in managing books for our institute. I have also had the opportunity of shopping for groceries and fulfilling the immediate and necessary needs of our sisters. I have also been attempting to instruct others in these "practical arts."

4. I have short term experience in working with the deaf — -instructing them in our faith. This past summer, at the workshop in Detroit, I was able to pick up some sign language and information on the psychology of the deaf and how to teach them. This also may be beneficial.

5. My actual experience in teaching religion is very limited as I have just begun to teach high school girls this subject this year. I believe that teaching religion, doing catechetical work, showing your interest and love for people through home visits, etc., is a vital part of religious life. I have been eager to do this kind of work, but up until now have not had much of an opportunity. I enjoy this work for through it I am working with the whole man and not just one part of him. While teaching skill subjects, I have gotten a very limited picture of man; the opportunity to get to know the whole man is not as great through subjects such as these. Because I have been interested in catechetical work and wanted the chance to attempt teaching religion, I

became engaged in teaching CCD (religion for Catholic students attending public schools) to the deaf. This, too, has taught me much and opened my vision and made me more aware of other people and their needs.

Mother, I don't know how coherent this letter is. My two main points that I am trying to get across are: 1) that I have a sincere love for and desire to help people—and for some reason the Spanish and Indian people do have a special appeal for me, and 2) I believe that catechetical work is an important part of religious life——one so important that I would venture to say that maybe religious life should revolve more closely around it.

Mother, please understand that I do see and realize the need we have for missionaries right here in Cleveland—and I am very happy to be a part of this work right now. If this is where you think I am most effective, I shall be very happy to continue on as such.

Thank you for your time and consideration.

God love you!

Sr. Dorothy Kazel

**Postulant Sr. Kazel with her only sibling,
Jim Kazel**

The following notes were found in Sr. Dorothy's retreat diaries. They underscore her commitment to her Ursuline vocation and her reliance on prayer as the solid basis for her growing spirituality.

August 7, 1963
MOTTO

I am an Ursuline. This is the ROOT of me. Everything else is secondary because I am an Ursuline. Therefore, there can be no MEDIOCRITY!

What is an Ursuline?

A woman in love. A nun dedicated to the work of SOLELY loving God through daily praise, reverence, and service.

How must I act as an Ursuline?

As one who knows and loves God, for this is my SPECIALTY and can be achieved through prayer. All I do must show this—for this is my life!

RESOLVE:

I desire to acquire a "spirit of prayer" which will eventually control my natural instincts, especially the desire to be esteemed, and have me prove myself as an Ursuline—a true LOVER of God.

CHATER 1: THE GROWING YEARS

Dorothy Chapon Kazel

Every one of us is given the "gift of life" at birth. It is what we do with this precious gift and how we use it that helps bring us peace and contentment. Life is a commitment. Sister Dorothy knew this. Sister Dorothy was an ordinary, everyday woman like you and me who lived an extraordinary life. I think what made Sister Dorothy outstanding was her ability to love life. She saw God's beauty in everyone and everything.

It was in her home, from her parents, that Dorothy received this attitude and positive approach to life. When she was a child, Dorothy made a striking appearance with her blonde hair, blue eyes and fair completion. She played the piano, was an avid athlete — excelling in baseball and was an excellent roller skater. I recall going one day with her to Skateland. There she took a nasty fall. Although she was bruised and ached all over, she got up without a murmur and started to skate once more. Dorothy was committed to learning how to master that figure eight. She not only mastered it but also went on to win many skating trophies. She was really committed to trying, to learning, to doing and to getting up and starting over.

Her total involvement in living life to the fullest was evident in everything she did such as: studding for an exam, going to a high school prom, starring in the play Cheaper by the Dozen and even picking strawberries in season. Basically, she was a young adult doing ordinary things. In fact she even fell in love and became engaged in 1959.

I know the engagement period was exciting for Dorothy in her life because the bridal party had been chosen, the wedding date was set for August 5, 1960 and arrangements for her honeymoon had been finalized.

During the courtship, Dorothy continued to live at home and teach at St. Robert's parochial school in Euclid, Ohio. It was during this period that Dorothy alone in her bedroom one evening had an unusual experience of the presence of God. It seemed as if her room was suffused in sunlight. Suddenly she realized that possibly she was not intended for marriage; perhaps God meant her to become a religious. If she were really called to become a sister, marriage was out of the picture. A retreat for Brides-To-Be was made at St. Joseph's Christian Life Center underscored the finality of this decision.

By returning the engagement ring she was free to take the first step toward religious life. It was on September 8, 1960 that she entered the Ursuline Novitiate. Throughout the novitiate, Dorothy deepened her knowledge of prayer, theology and secular studies.

When Dorothy was clothed in the religious habit, she received the name Sister Laurentine which was the name of one of the Ursuline nuns who had been martyred during the French Revolution. Later, Sister Dorothy resumed the use of her baptismal name Dorothy. This resulted in some confusion with me because I then was married to her only brother and had acquired the family name. This made both of us Dorothy Kazel. We laughed about this and at one time thought of going on the television show TO TELL THE TRUTH and thought how comical it would be when the master of ceremonies might ask: Will the real Dorothy Kazel please stand!"

Sister Dorothy graduated on June 1, 1965 from Ursuline College, Pepper Pike, Ohio and was assigned to teach at Sacred Heart Academy and later at Beaumont High School for girls in Cleveland, Heights, and Ohio. In the dual capacity of teacher-counselor, Sister Dorothy worked untiringly with many students who remember her with love and gratitude.

I would like to share some students' thoughts about Sister Dorothy. One stated: "I always thought sisters were born nuns until I met Dorothy. She was the first nun to let me see her human side. Her humanness as a fun loving person deepened my faith."

That young people had a special place in their hearts for Dorothy can be seen in what another student stated: "Sister Dorothy had a reputation among us students for being someone with whom we could talk. To me she seemed to be the IDEAL nun. She did not let her attempt to be "holy" interfere with her being a human, with being a woman."

Personally, I believe through her teaching, she showed her students that she truly cared about them and was able to bring out their qualities through imitation of her Christian principles. They must have sensed her inner peace, and serenity, too, as she listened to them and helped them solve their own problems, and by her encouragement affirmed them in their faithfulness.

As a young professed Sister, Dorothy was gaining many new experiences to prepare for a new ministry. She taught CCD, studied methods to teach the deaf, and volunteered to spend a summer in Arizona teaching the Papago Indians. These and other experiences were invaluable when her request to go to El Salvador was answered.

As a follower of St. Angela Merici the foundress of the Ursuline Order who placed great emphases on the education of women, Sister Dorothy graduated from John Carroll University in 1974 obtaining a master's degree in counseling.

Enjoying success as an educator, accepted and appreciated by students and faculty, Dorothy still harbored in her heart the desire to become a missionary in Central America. Her dream became a reality when on July 29, 1974; she was given an assignment to El Salvador for a five-year term.

The Diocese of Cleveland had established a mission in El Salvador back in 1964. The Ursuline general superior asked for volunteers from among the nuns and Dorothy was among the first to offer her services to the Cleveland Mission Team.

I will never forget when she surprised me with a visit to my home one afternoon. I made us a cup of tea and then she told me the news that she was becoming a missionary. Our eyes swelled with tears. I sat there pondering how Sister Dorothy was facing a challenging commitment on the other side of the continent and I was handling one within the confines of my home raising my six children. How different, yet similar were our goals, but we both shared the belief that life is love and commitment.

Now that her dream and commitment had become a reality she had to prepare for this work by attending the Language Institute in Santa Jose, Costa Rica.

From Costa Rico she was assigned to a parish in Chirilagua, one of the areas in which the Cleveland Team carried out their ministry in El Salvador. From there she went to the parish San Carlos Borromeo in La Union and finally to the parish of the Immaculate Conception in the port of La Libertad.

One of Dorothy's colleagues recalls that the first impression Dorothy made on the mission team was the intensity of her light heartedness. They felt that her light heartedness reflected a deep joy and peace that she was experiencing within. They found Dorothy very open to new ideas, to the new and challenging cultural perspectives. She was able to let go of her cultural biases to hear with new ears, to see with new eyes the story of the poor and oppressed peoples of El Salvador. Not all missionaries find it that easy to step into the shoes of Third World peoples and let go of their First World mentality. She was a living embodiment of her favorite quote from St. Augustine; "A Christian should be an Alleluia person from head to foot."

She had a great depth to her and was such a clown and so light hearted that at times you might think she wasn't taking things seriously. She truly respected each person even though some thought differently from her. She didn't impose her ideas on them. That does not mean that she was a pushover. She had strong convictions and would stand by them. She was not threatened by others viewpoints no matter how strongly they presented them. She could act freely, with ease because she knew who she was. She was not trying to make points, be a climber, or a pleaser. She could recognize manipulative ways and stand her ground.

Dorothy was a very prayerful person, and I know that she fasted once a week. She integrated her prayer life with her daily living and service to others. Truly she was an "Alleluia from head to foot."

Reflecting on that statement I think the following words describe her: Fun loving, dedicated, generous, prayerful, vibrant, youthful, refreshing, energetic, enthusiastic, free, intelligent, capable and relational.

In her first letter home she described the beauty of the country and the simplicity of the people. A journal notation for Monday, July 29, 1974 states: "Arrived in San Salvador and the entire team met us. Had a coke in the terminal and chatted. Drove to Chirilagua, had supper, got to bed after midnight. Awakened 4:00 am by serenaders (beautiful)."

On Wednesday July 31 she journaled: "At 9:15 am went with Rosemary Smith to meeting with women in Caritas program. Ate "corn starch soup" and corn. Then went over to Pacific and swam. Warm and wonderful? Dear little girl – Lelia – there. Poverty great but God's beauty in abundance! Came home, washed, rested, Mass 7:00pm."

Dorothy soon found herself immersed in a whirlwind of activities: preparation of native lay persons as catechists; instruction of woman in basic nutrition, food preparation, hygiene, and child care; instruction of children for the reception of the sacraments; conducting a choir, arranging for liturgies and visiting the sick.

"Love does make the world go 'round-and also helps to make it a better place to live in" wrote Dorothy in one of the CLAM (Cleveland Latin American Mission) letters. "An organization called Caritas El Salvador meaning LOVE, founded in 1960, helped fight against the prevalent malnutrition and lack of education. For a small fee the program supplements the Salvadorans regular diet of tortillas, rice, and beans. The fee accents the fact that it is not just a "handout" and helps the people to safeguard their self-respect. Caritas fundamentally is an extension of the love of other people in other countries for the poor in El Salvador."

My sister-in-law invited me to visit her in Salvador numerous times, always reassuring me that "the moving earth down there has not been bad lately" Further stating: "We've had a couple tremors-but nothing exciting so don't worry about it. California will go before Central America!"

My gutsy sister-in-saw lived through earthquakes, ate beans and tortias, took attempted suicide victims to the hospitals, removed knifed victims from the main streets, endured the heat and mosquitoes, fought malaria and dysentery and stayed in El Salvador for five and a half years. She was committed to the people and her church.

The political unrest increased the duties of Dorothy and her companions considerably in 1977 as stated in her letter home to us: "This unrest has affected our work in that most of it must now be carried out during the afternoon instead of the evening when more people would be free to come. We've each been personally affected by what we see around us as a result of suspicion, rumor; fear, threat and people's coping mechanisms."

Amid the misery, violence, and confusion enveloping the country, Archbishop Romero served as a beacon to light the way toward peace and justice for his people. Under his leadership, the Catholic Church of El Salvador stood shoulder to shoulder with the poor and the oppressed. Dorothy regarded him as a vital champion of peace and justice.

Dorothy continued her daily routine working with orphans, widows, the aged, babies and children... I believe her commitment grew stronger because of the violence. It was a Civil War. She definitely was needed to help the refugees and wounded.

I think I understand why she went back and died there in a patch of beauty. It was essential for her to return because her commitment to care for the needs of others by peaceful methods not guns or bullets. To be able to look people in the eyes and extend a loving arm or an assuring hand on the shoulder. She cared deeply about the people. So this is a time of remembering.

CHAPTER 2: THE EARLY MISSION YEARS THE LETTERS OF 1974 - 1976

Dorothy's First Days in Central America

*N*otice Dorothy's transition from tourist to resident and eventually to full participant in mission life! Of particular interest to the reader could be the last letter of this section dated May 10, 1976 which tells us of her ideas resulting in five projects for the benefit of her people. These included books for a traveling library purchase of fertilizer for farmers, and a girls' vocation project.

Tues. 7-30-74

Dear Mom & Dad,

We made it in one piece; the team met us at the airport. After eating, we headed to Chirilagua. After getting to bed after midnight, we were awakened at

4:00 a.m. by our serenading church group. It was really lovely.

We then slept to about 10:00, got up, "showered" in our birdhouse, and ate at the priest's house. They took us around Chirilagua today (a very poor place). We then went to Mass at Candlera, another poor village and then had Mass here again at 7:00 – by candlelight, as it rained and knocked out the electricity!

All is going well – there is much to see and learn. Will write again.

Love - Dorothy

Sun 8–10–74

Dear Mom & Dad,

How are you? Hope all is well with you!

I want you to know I received your letter with the "dollar test" but the others here said that's too risky - a check is safer because they often steal mail. It does take us a good week to get the mail from home – it might be quicker getting it up to Cleveland. Have you found that?

Did you get my tape? I hope so. Thought you would enjoy it – Jim & Dorth, too – and maybe Sever. I just sent one to Beaumont this week. Maybe you could "swap" with them later.

I picked up a little purse for Celeste – hope she likes it!

Could you distribute these "goods" for me, please!

We're leaving for Costa Rica on Aug. 24 – by plane. The only address I have right now is the school:

Take care – Write when you can! Love – Your daughter

Aug. 12, 1974

Hi Mom & Dad!

...We had our first team meeting today–all the people from here, La Libertad, & La Union get together to discuss what's happening in each of the parishes. It really is interesting! Afterward, we took a dip in the Bay–'twas great–and warm

Take care–miss you!

Love, your daughter

By now, Dorothy and Martha are enrolled for further studies in Spanish in Costa Rica.

9-2-74

Hi Mom & Dad!

...We had our first full day of classes today. T'was interesting – but taxes the brain because it's a lot of drill and memorizing. However, that seems to be the only way to learn.

Sr. Martha got a tape today from her family – her mom and dad have a Spanish book and are trying to learn a few words. They're a hoot! Have you tried taping yet? Please do – just record over my tape and send it back. It would be good to hear you, too...

Hope you had a relaxing Labor Day –

Take care –
Love –
Your daughter

APARTADO 10240 – SAN JOSE – COSTA RICA
Tues. 9-10-74

Dear Mom & Dad –

...I just came back from San Jose. I bought you a gold coin. It's really tiny – slightly smaller than dime size. This man said the value is not in the gold (as it contains maybe 2 gram) but in the coin itself. It is a Costa Rican coin – 1900 – DOS COLONES or 2 colones. Maybe you know somebody you can ask about it. I paid $20 for it. He showed me another slightly larger one, which was $50, but for some reason, it just didn't look authentic to me –beside, that was out of my budget! To buy gold of any nature, even minimal amounts, runs in the $100's and up. Also, I don't know anything about it – let alone these coins – so I wouldn't know if I was getting the real thing or not. Anyway, you're going to have to wait to get this cuz I don't want to put it I the mail, ok?

School is still rough. We're going out to eat tomorrow with a group of gals from school – celebrating a birthday of one. Sound familiar??? We may go to our Swiss Chalet – really has delicious food.

Got to do some work – so take care. Hope all is well!

Love ya!
your daughter

Sunday 9-15-74

Hola Mom & Dad!

How are you? Hope all is well! Is this the weekend you went to Niagara Falls? Hope you had good weather!

Today we took another "happy trip" with these 2 ladies we met last Sunday – Maria & Connie. They took us up to the Volcano Poas. The road to it was unbelievable. Really, it's the worst I've been on for curves – and being one lane – wow! We went way up into the mountains – 'twas beautiful! And cold. The crater was quite fog-filled so we didn't see too much. It also has a sulphur stench coming from it – but not real strong. We walked up to this other crater area that was water-filled. That was beautiful – very green.

Before heading for the crater, we saw several parades. Today is their Independence Day – and every school marches! So we kept running into groups all the way up. You know I just got an idea. The price of film here is almost $5 a roll – and developing is also expensive. Right now I'm using slides. Do you still send in your film to be developed somewhere? If so, why don't you send me one of their envelopes so I can try mailing it in. It might be cheaper, ok?

Also, we went to the leather factory again. Would Dad, Jim, and David use a belt if I bought them one – or don't they like wide ones or narrow ones – any particular color? What about waist sizes?

Also Mother, I debated about a purse for you –
would you like one? With a "tooled" design or plain?
Let me know what you would like, ok?

Have to get some studying in. Do take care –
write when you can. Oh, the "pebbles" are from the
Volcano!

Miss ya & Love ya! your daughter

*Maria Del Carmen Bolanz who is mentioned in this
letter worked with the missionaries in Chirilagua and
quickly became a good friend to Dorothy. She is now
a teacher of Spanish in Cleveland, Ohio. The first
Christmas letter reflects a caring Dorothy sending
gifts to parents and nieces and nephews. She also
sent little volcanic rocks in her letters.*

Sunday 9-21-74

Hola!

I certainly received a happy surprise on Friday
– I finally got a tape from you with your voices on.
That was great! Thanks so much. That first part was a
hoot – all you could make out was everyone laughing
and having a good time. Sorry I wasn't there!

I'm just finishing a tape for Patty – then I'll begin
one for you again.

Today was a beautiful day – and we went with
our lady friends to Volcano Iragu. T'was beautiful
– and clear. You could see all the way into the crater.
The bottom was a pea-green lake. It really was large
– gave an overpowering feeling. The last time it
erupted was in 1964. The volcano we saw last week
(Poad) was much larger but you couldn't see anything

cuz we were in a cloud. But this past week, it "spit up" a few things. The enclosed articles tell about it.

Today's mountain scenery was the most beautiful yet – I'm sure it even beats "The Sound of Music" We stopped at some peoples house to eat – really sweet, simple country folk who live up on this mountain from which you can see so many beautiful sights. We're invited back Oct. 20 to celebrate Maria's birthday and have some corn. So...this coming week we're also invited to eat out on Thursday & Friday. At least we won't starve!

Also enclosed you will find a crushed flower – they grow on trees around here and are just beautiful!

Take care – will begin your tape soon! God love you! Love – your daughter
PS-Don't send me the rosary – just continue to say it
    for me! Thanks!

Jim and David, who are mentioned in the following letter, are Sr. Dorothy's brother and nephew. Cheryl, Colleen and Celeste are her nieces.

                                   11 – 15 – 74

Dear Mom & Dad!

Merry Christmas, Happy Thanksgiving, Happy Easter, etc!!!

I think this is the last batch of "goodies" coming as once I get to Salvador; it's not so easy to mail things.

Anyway – the purse is "typical" for you, Mom. Inside are belts for Dad, David, & Jim, which are not real typical – but I do hope they fit – and can use them. They, and your purse were bought at the leather factory here in Moravia, Costa Rica. There are 3 coin purses for Cheryl, Colleen, & Celeste with a charm & 15 centinos inside (equivalent to about 2 American cents – wow! It looks like "play money" but it's actually what we use here. Maybe you remember me saying we pay 35 centinos to ride the bus (about 4 ½ cents) and our letters are 85 centinos (9 – 10 cents) – but US. Mail rates are going up Dec. 1 to 19 American cents. I just hope that doesn't happen in Salvador!!!

Anyway, I also sent a package to Jim's house with a blouse for Dorth and shirts for Dan & Jamie. Hope all this gets to you people ok!

Take care – will write again. Love – your daughter

11 – 18 – 74

Hola!

Got your tape today – thanks so much. Was good to hear you again. Mom, that was a 2-hour tape, too. When you want to finish up a tape, just put it by your FM radio – we always like to hear good music, ok?

I went to the dentist today to get a "fallen out filling" replaced – she (the dentist) really was nice. Listen to Jim's tape to get the details, ok? Anyway, while I was in town I bought some of these slides of C.R. *(Costa Rica)*, which were cheap – and nice, I thought. So please hold onto them for me. Did my pictures get to you yet?? Hope they come soon.

Our mail has been taking about 8 days to get here – how is it with you? Anyway – I better say HAPPY

THANKSGIVING, now. I will call on that day. Take care!

Much love - your daughter

"Barb" is Barb Sever who taught with S. Dorothy at Beaumont High School in Cleveland. Later, Barb entered the Ursuline Sisters.

Monday, 11 – 25 – 74

Greetings!

Got your letter with $5 enclosed ok – Thanks so much as I really am getting "low" after this Panama trip. 'Twas fun – the section of Panama City we were in was a "bargain basement" area. I bought 3 blouses @ 99 cents each – and they're kind of nice - something like you'd get in K-Mart or Uncle Bills. We also saw the American side of the Canal Zone – kind of made you homesick cuz it was so much like the U.S. The "lock" where the ships pass thru was really fantastic. Will tell you more on the tape.

Three more weeks of school – yippee! Can't believe it! Time does go quickly.

Am happy Father is doing well. That's great! Barb sent me a tape & tells me she sees you everyday. That's nice.

Got to go to bed, as I'm exhausted. Will talk with you on Thursday!

Take care –
Love –
Your daughter

Most of the letters from 1975 are brief notes usually accompanying audio tapes or gift packages. About half way into 1976, this particular letter appears with specific information on the work the team is doing and the projects undertaken. It is written to the Ursuline community back home in Cleveland with a humorous note to the Mother Superior, Mother Annunciata, mentioning the "guilt" Dorothy and Martha felt for not having written sooner to acknowledge their gratitude for the money sent to them by the order's silver jubilarian class of that year. They describe how the generosity of the jubilarians helped create their projects, the parish lending co-operative and the traveling library and a reading program.

May 10, 1976

Dear Mother and all,

We feel a little guilty about not writing sooner – so we made up a good long letter- mostly explaining how we used the jubilee money. Hope all is going well.

It's been ages since we've written you, so before school is out and the elections are upon us we'd like to share with you what we've been up to.

Since our work is pastoral you will find that it is very much like work at home — yet it's quite different. We're sure most of you know we live in a city (La Union just got daily water in April!) but we also work in small farm villages. Perhaps most of our working time is spent at the latter in a basic doctrine program we bring to the farmers. We also work closely with the priests helping them form community and celebrating the sacraments in these small cantons. There is also a large group of teenagers we meet with regularly and a group of women leaders for whom we are responsible. We also serve as links between the priests and the catechist conveying messages and getting needed materials. First Communion in the city is probably as big as any place back home and will be June 20 this year. There is also the continual jobs of learning new songs. Working with the choir, cleaning the house (we have help but with the dust the work never seems to be done!), cooking once a week, weekly and monthly meetings, etc.

We also have a new addition to our family. Sister Christine Rody a Vincentian sister from Bedford, Ohio joined us in February. She is spending two weeks in La Libertad for In-Service training right now — but is happily adjusting to the life and climate here in La Union.

There are also 5 new projects we've launched off into. The first one is a Vocation Program for Girls we've been planning for almost six months now. We think we are sure of three vocations for the native communities right now. We hope our new group will produce many more.

Projects 2 to 5 are due to the generosity of the 25th Jubilarians so we've named them Projecto Plata — or "Silver Project". In Project 2, Projecto Plata, we were able to purchase 96 books with $200 of their money for our Traveling Library. On discounts we saved $30 which we used to buy carrying cases and plastic bags (it rains inside these houses). We have six cases ready to go for one month to a canton. All are catalogued (our own system). At the end of the month the cases will rotate. We're very excited and the people are very anxious for us to begin.

Project 3, Projecto Plata, is perhaps our biggest—it deals with $1,000 that we put into the parish lending cooperative. Not only will the money be lent to buy fertilizer but we have purchased the fertilizer at a reduced price as an additional savings to the campesino (farmer). We have renounced any dividends we might gain in the Cooperative and have instructed that they be divided among the members. Thus the 2% interest will be divided among the members of the Cooperative who are the same borrowers, and our catechists. They gain in all ways. We also are praying that with good growing weather they will be able to turn their investment into food and money worth ten times the original investment. We'll try to get sample figures as the growing season progresses.

Project 4, Projecto Plata, deals with a reading and writing program called Alfalit. We are going to use $100 as support money for the program mostly as aid to the volunteer teachers who give the classes.

We know perhaps better than any Ursuline how important these contributions are to the lives of our 51,000 parishioners whom we are trying to help realize their full dignity as persons, new persons capable of reaching full development through their ability to read and write. This will make accessible to them the ways of learning and the rich possession of truth, both human and divine, that we enjoy. We hope to help them become men who can "rule the earth", that is to say, men who are able to tame the land and put it at the service of humanity.

Almost half of our parishioners live on the Volcano Conchagua or one of our three islands. It is almost impossible to reach some of them but you can trust us to do our best to help wherever we can. It is beautiful here. We are watching "new men" being born every day. In the name of these "new men" we wish to thank all Ursulines for our presence here and especially the 25th Jubilarians for Projecto Plata.

As long as thanks are in order, we should like to extend a public expression of our gratitude to Mother Annunciata for her personal concern for us over the last two years—and also her first mandate of two Ursulines in 1968. Quite honestly, we have felt privileged to serve here in El Salvador under her leadership. Without a doubt she has been our most important community contact; and, we might add, our treasured friend.

And so we continue, living through earthquakes, eating beans and tortillas in the cantons, taking attempted suicide victims to the hospital, walking in dust or water up to our ankles (depends on the season), removing knifed victims from the main streets, building houses, demolishing and rebuilding churches, enduring the heat and mosquitoes, fighting malaria and dysentery and just generally having a great time in the name of the Ursulines and the Christ who is Lord! God Love You All!

Our love and prayers—

Sister Dorothy

Throughout her religious life, but especially while serving in El Salvador, Sr. Dorothy practiced the mortification of fasting at least one day a week. She believed in the spiritual strength one achieved through this practice.

DOROTHY'S GROWING SPIRITUALITY: A DAY OF FAST

Dorothy Chapon Kazel

Vividly, I recall one of Sister Dorothy's annual visits from El Salvador. After embracing, we noticed changes in each other. I had gained a couple of pounds, she had shed a few and was trim and toned. After pleasant chatter, our conversation turned towards fasting. Chuckling, she mentioned that besides possible physical improvements that go with fasting, the opportunity exists to expand spiritual horizons. In addition to being a solution to over-indulging, Dorothy offered me new insights on spiritual discipline. The purpose of fasting, she explained, was to deny the needs of the body; in essence, denial is good and pleasing to God when done in a holistic manner. Her inspirational adage was: "Learning to say no develops strength." Further, we discussed how the saints of centuries past partook in true fasting. They possessed an awakened spiritual consciousness and focused their gaze on God alone. Their hope was invested in freeing the oppressed and providing bread for the hungry.

Sister Dorothy's personal day for fasting was Saturday. On this day she would only drink juice. Her faith in God, expressed in a day of fast, made such an impact on me. By no means would Dorothy want me to call her a saint because her motivation to fast was not self-enhancing; fasting was not a self-interest project to loose weight, but rather for Sister Dorothy it was a sacrifice done for the love of another human being. Through denial, she felt she could more freely and joyfully cleave to God.

Her spiritual fasting was deeply rooted in emulating the lives of saints. For example, leafing through some journals, I found a quotation of hers on mortification. Dated August 3, 1961, written during a Retreat by Reverend Henry Birkenhauer, S.J. "Mortification equals a means of development...to 'tuffin', spiritual life...Mortification is an outpouring of love."

Sister Dorothy was a woman of her times. She was a contemporary woman of the church with a deep, abiding spirituality best expressed in a lived faith. Even in the 20th century, she truly believed in fasting one day a week. Her fast would often be for a friend. Dorothy's motivation was not for self-interest but focused on the concerns of the suffering.

Like the saints of centuries past her hope was to free the oppressed and to provide bread for the hungry.

CHAPTER 3. THE MATURING YEARS: THE LETTERS OF 1977-1979

Sr. Mary Ann Flannery, SC

The letters between 1976 and 1979 are simple narratives of a Dorothy Kazel growing in mission life. They are brief documents that provide only a very limited insight into the work she and the missionaries were doing. However, as seen in the last letter of 1976, a careful mentioning of danger and death begins to seep into these messages home. One also sees how the awareness of this danger adds a sober tenor to the letters which now focus more on pastoral activities. More than likely, the tapes, sent to her family and friends, were fuller with the details and challenges of her work.

There are fewer letters during this period of time because the audiotapes became the missioners' main form of communication. The characteristics of these letters are three-fold. First, they are light in style with little dependence on detail almost as if Dorothy had limited time in which to write since she was narrating so much on the tapes. Second, the letters reflect a thoughtful Dorothy, one who would attach a short letter with her tape almost out of courtesy or loyalty. Third, these letters express very little of the El Salvador Dorothy was coming to know as the political climate was beginning to intensify between the military government and the guerilla opposition. Instead, Dorothy concentrates on what she may have thought would interest her family and friends: missionary parties, visitors to the mission, sightseeing trips, etc. According to those who worked with her, these non-disclosing letters involved two objectives which grew out of Dorothy's concern for others. She did not want to worry her readers and she feared the interception of mail by Salvadoran authorities which could have endangered team members and anyone associated with them. Thus, the tapes were "safer" forms of communication.

Nonetheless, these years are the maturing missionary years for Sr. Dorothy Kazel. Toward the end of this period, 1978-1979, the letters get longer because they were sent by mail. During this time Cleveland Bishop James A. Hickey discouraged casual visits to the team because of mounting dangers so the tapes became a less frequent form of communication.

Of this period one can detect a faint apprehension of the political climate. A particularly informative letter is sent to Dorothy's General Superior, Mother

Mary Bartholomew in 1977 and is the first indication of concern though—as Dorothy wrote; ". we are not in any immediate danger," a definite attempt to down-play the tensions by now fairly rampant throughout El Salvador.

By 1977, Sr. Dorothy Kazel and Sr. Martha Owen were stationed in Zaragoza along with Sr. Christine Rody, also a Clevelander and a Vincentian Sister of Charity. The missionaries are focused on their work, a large part of which was the Caritas program explained in Dorothy's letter of June 1977. As the months wore on, however, the dangers increased.

Correspondence picks up in 1979 when Dorothy settles into her fourth assignment, the port city of La Libertad. By now, Dorothy and Martha have completed their four year term and their superior, Mother Bartholomew McCaffery, and their Bishop, James A. Hickey of Cleveland, begin to discuss the possibility of one of the two Ursulines to remain in order to assist new missionaries who are coming into a volatile situation. Mother Bartholomew and her council ask the two missionaries to decide between themselves as to who should remain. Sister Martha and Sister Dorothy decide the latter should remain because of her work in transporting refugees and her positive working relationship with Jean Donovan, a newly arrived missionary in the Port. Martha, on the other hand, was still serving in Zaragoza with Ken and Chris, fairly seasoned missionaries who knew what to expect and how to react.

Martha, Dorothy's good friend and confidant, left El Salvador in 1979, her time having been completed.

According to the plan devised with Bishop Hickey, Dorothy was to leave sometime in 1980.

According to Pannikar, orthopoesis is a time in which the person's growth relies on a relationship with God that has so internalized the individual's dedication to a cause or way of life that the person moves toward. At this time of her life, Dorothy is not "there" in her spiritual development. But she is on her way. Her love for the people and culture of El Salvador, along with the camaraderie of a hard-working, generous missionary team, have challenged her intuitive inclination toward serving the poor. While she is apparently happy and dedicated, the political world of El Salvador is making inroads into her simple life and she is working on closing it out as if to focus purely on the peoples' needs that she can address.

The following letters written by the Cleveland Mission Team begin to show us the real political situation of El Salvador at this time.

CLAM – CLEVELAND LATIN AMERICAN
MISSION EL SALVADOR C.A.

February, 1977

Dear Friends Back Home:

Warm greetings from hot, sunny El Salvador! How we wish we could send you a bit of our weather. Local newspapers here have devoted considerable space—even first-page three-inch headlines- to describe in detail how seriously "la ola de frio" (the cold wave) has damaged the eastern and Great Lakes areas of the USA. We hope and pray that by the time you read this letter, the worst will have passed and you will be looking forward to a pleasant spring.

Doubtless you have seen the <u>Universe-Bulletin</u> (UB the Catholic newspaper of Cleveland) of January 21, with its full page entitled, "Cleveland Missionaries in Latin America Depend on You..." The diocesan mission director, Father John Garrity, sent us this special page, and also a clipped news article telling about the "shooting" that went on down here in early December. We who are involved in all this read with great interest that the new thirty-minute film on the Cleveland Diocese missions in El Salvador is expected to be ready for viewing by March, and possibly on local TV also. We hope that you, our friends and benefactors, will have an opportunity to see, <u>live</u>, in this movie some of the wonderful results made possible by your own caring and support.

Your children in school will have an opportunity to see a film strip, "Signs of Hope", with accompanying lesson guides prepared by Sister Therese Mary Osborn, OSU. Private donations financed these productions.

On the full page of the UB, you recognized by name if not by the "mug shots", those of us whom you know personally. Many of you also know the other Cleveland Diocese folks whose names are listed as serving in various missions in Latin America. Your names, too, deserve to be listed among those who give "Witness of Solidarity", as this same page affirms. Your concern, expressed in prayer and financial support, gives a witness just as authentic as we trust ours is.

We could not do without you. Our programs designed to help the poor, the oppressed and the persecuted in Latin America are funded by your continuing donations, large and small. Without your generous support we could not carry on the projects and programs offered by team members in our scattered parishes in El Salvador: catechist and leadership training for both men and women, all important in this priest-short country; sacramental preparation; education in nutrition and health; all this in addition to meeting other spiritual and liturgical needs.

These lovable, appreciative Salvadorans cannot thank you personally but they thank you sincerely through us. We thank you, too, for enabling us to help "El Salvador", (the Savior) continue his sublime mission of evangelization in this beautiful land bearing his name. As Father Garrity said, "Our diocese's care and concern is their hope for tomorrow." May God bless all of you in this year of hope, 1977.

With love in "El Salvador",
The Cleveland Mission Team

Dorothy enclosed personal notes to her community with every tape or packages of mail sent to Cleveland. As her sister-in-law, I can't imagine how I would have felt had I read some of these letters sent back to the Ursulines. This particular letter responds to the superior's request that Dorothy and Martha consider some of the end-of-life wishes which the community should have on file in the event of death of either missionary.

Feb. 4, 1977

Dear Mother and Council,

By now you've probably had the chance to talk to Martha if you haven't seen her. I sure hope she doesn't freeze too badly in Cleveland — your weather sounds fierce!

Thank you for the letters we've received lately. The one was regarding place of burial. I haven't really discussed this with my family — but sensibly speaking, I think it would be much easier to bury me here than to transport a body home. Hopefully, we'll never have to actually go through with this.

One slight problem is this. Today, I just received a brown envelope with a couple Christmas cards and info on the Summer Workshop. It was sent Dec. 13 but NOT marked AIRMAIL. That is all-important otherwise it just goes regular and takes forever to get here. So...please put on the airmail. Thanks.

As of now, we're still not settled on where we'll be moving – or when Fr. Jim McCreight is home on vacation and will talk with Bishop Hickey about the future. Since he will be returning to the states for good, his departure date will influence us. Again, you will probably know before us just what will be happening.

Do take care – don't freeze! And keep us in your prayers. We will be in Guatemala Feb. 12 – March 12.

Love — S. Dorothy
October 1978

CLAM - Cleveland Latin American Mission
Dear Friends back home,

Every one back home is getting settled into the pattern of the new school year. Here in El Salvador our school year is winding down. The catechetical centers have difficulty in enrolling men and women because they are leaving their homes to make their yearly income by harvesting coffee, sugar cane and cotton. Even the children in the Parroquial School at La Libertad are preparing to go with their parents to earn the few pennies that they can in order to augment their parents meager income.

However, this year we have reason that we can praise the Lord. The rains this year have been plentiful and the harvests are excellent. Fr. Bill says that it is the best he has seen in all his years down here.

As all are aware of the situation in Nicaragua, much of Latin America is reaping another kind of harvest - the harvest of many years of social injustice. Here in El Salvador the powerful leaders continue to ignore the prophetic voice of our loved Archbishop Oscar Romero and still try to force even greater oppression over our people. It is like throwing gasoline on fire to put it out.

One ray of hope looks towards the third conference of Latin American Bishops, which is to be held in Pueblo Mexico during the month of October. Here the bishops of Latin America will be praying and working, asking the lord for paths through the complex labyrinth of social evil which plague Latin America.

During these days we again ask your prayers and sacrifices for us, our work and most important our people that under the protection of the Virgin of Guadalupe, the patroness of Latin and North America, the kingdom of God may be more firmly established in these days. God bless you and your family;

The Cleveland Mission Team

Dorothy mentions that a new "prospective" will arrive soon—Jean Donovan. Jean, a young accountant with Arthur Anderson's office in Cleveland, Ohio, is discerning whether to join the team and give a year or more to the church. Jean was also thinking of marriage but decided, with her fiancé, to wait until her missionary experience was complete before making wedding plans.

The letter to Mother Bartholomew narrates some of the increasing tension Dorothy was experiencing with the government. She mentions the call from the embassy warning the missionaries not to travel to the capital. She closes with thoughts of her future— possibly more education on the challenge of being a Christian facing the effects of capitalism and society. She seems to have entered that period of spiritual development which Panikkar calls "orthopeoesis". In the expansion of her awareness of the militaristic and tyrannical government forces taking hold in El Salvador, she begins to see a need to learn more in order to place herself on the side of advocacy for the poor.

October 1

Greetings to all!

Just think – in a short time we'll be seeing you – that's great. Hopefully, our rains will have ceased by then – we've really had lots. Just last night we had a couple tragedies. A landslide with huge boulders completely demolished a home and 5 children. Also, a lady got carried out in a river and her body has not been found yet – so please keep our people in your prayers.

We are all fine here – our yard sometimes looks like a mud lake – but that's about all. It's quite different from when Sr. James Francis was here. It actually even gets cool here – maybe 70 or even 68 degrees. So – be prepared.

Oh, please excuse the letter on the other side. Fr. Paul did it all by himself. We must remember <u>NOT</u> to let him type it again!

A Jean Donovan is coming down Oct. 10 to visit. She's a "prospective" missionary—so we shall see what happens.

Mother, thank you, too, for taking care of Maria del Carmen – we really appreciate that.

Do take care all – We'll see you soon!

Love & prayers —-S Dorothy & Martha

The friend in the following letter is Sister Martha Owens, OSU who had already completed her time in El Salvador and had returned to the states. With gripping yet subtle innuendo of a portentous event, Dorothy has come full circle from a once carefree mission life to one facing the very real possibility –every day- of death. The reference to "Al" is to Fr. Alfred Winters, Director of the Mission Office in Cleveland and the Bishop's representative in charge of the Mission Team. Fr. Al personally delivered this letter to Martha Owen on his return home.

October 23, 1979

Dear Friend,

We had a good meeting today followed by a swim and a beautiful Liturgy. We are now getting ready to go out to eat.

Before I have to give this to Al, I do want to say something to you – I think you will understand. We talked quite a bit today about what happens IF something begins. And Most of us feel we would want to stay here. Now this depends on WHAT happens- if there is a way we can help – like run a Refugee Center or something, we wouldn't want to just run out on the people. Anyway, Al thinks people we love should understand how we feel – in case something happens – so he and the Bishop don't have to yank us out of there unnecessarily. Any way – I thought I should say this to you – cuz I don't want to say it to anyone else – cuz I don't think they would understand. Anyway, my beloved friend, just know how I feel and "treasure it in your heart." If a day comes when others will have to understand, please explain it for me—thanks. Love ya lots, D

"Mother" is Sister M. Bartholomew McCaffrey, the Superior of the Cleveland Ursuline sisters. This letter spells out the developing dangerous situation.

November 8, 1979

Dear Mother,

It certainly has been a while since I've written you—and I'm sorry about that. Much has been happening –but we are all fine, so please don't worry. We have been in contact with Fr. Al Winters—if we were in any serious danger I'm sure he would let you know. I hope to fill you in on just what has been happening and how we feel about the situation.

First of all when Fr. Winters came down to visit at the end of September we had some interesting discussions about our situation. Many times we joke about it, but he wanted to know that if worse came to worse, just what would we do. After sincere sharing of opinions most of us decided that we would definitely want to stay here to be with the people and help them in whatever way we could. Maybe some of this was influenced by the Maryknoll Sisters that we know quite well who were in the war in Nicaragua. During that time they ran a "refugee center" in Leon—and since then have given us lists of things to have ready for our potential refugee centers here. For instance the school in La Libertad would be an ideal place— and possibly the church in Zaragoza. Anyway, this is how we are thinking right now. If the situation were one where it would be impossible to do anything— and our lives would be more endangered than useful, we would probably consider leaving. It's just that normally speaking, when the chips are completely down, you can't just walk out on the people you've been working with. And we all feel that way. I hope you can understand this. Now this is not something we are HOPING to face; rather hopefully we will not have to do any of this. But it is something one has to have thought about beforehand.

Now the story on the Coup. On October 15, I took a group of Catechists out to Castano for a course. Afterward I went to Chirilagua for lunch. (Christine was in the states at this time and Jean (our new lay missioner) was in New Orleans with her family.) At noon, Rosie received a phone call from the U.S. Embassy saying there was shooting going on in the capital and if you didn't urgently have to go there, it were better not to go. We turned on the radio to find some news. The only thing we could pick up is that there had been some trouble in 4 cuartels in 4 different cities. So we decided to relax and go for a quick swim. When we came back I decided I'd better leave. It was about 4:15 and I didn't want to get home too late. Well, while driving I had the radio on but couldn't find out anything more. Around 6:00 p.m. I got to Zacatecaluca—and that's where I got stopped. You couldn't go any further. The entrance to San Salvador was blocked. The soldier told me he didn't know WHEN it would be opened again and maybe I should stay at the hotel for the night. So I went into the city and called Paul and told him my predicament and then headed back to Chirilagua. It was then that I heard on the radio that President Romero had abandoned the country and gone to Guatemala and that a new Junta had taken over! What a surprise!

The next morning I left Chirilagua about 11:00 a.m. and got back to the Port without any trouble. Interdepartmental driving had been prohibited in the night but there were no problems during the day. Also, the absence of policeman, army, guardia, etc. was astounding. The other surprising thing was that they had an interview with Monsignor Romero (not related to the President), on the radio. He expressed his surprise and concern that a coup had taken place so quietly—and better yet—without bloodshed. He said that the promises made by the new Junta were hopeful and that the populace should give them a change to prove themselves. I thought this very interesting because if Mons. Romero was speaking like this, they can't be all bad—because that's the way you would normally think—they're just another group of military men in charge. Anyway, since then, it sounds as if you've been getting quite a bit of news about what's going on down here.

The new Junta—composed of 2 military men and 3 civilians—have been trying to get on top of all situations and have been having a very hard time because many of the people here do not yet support them. Neither do the military and security forces. And these are the people who are causing the trouble. Someone just said that no revolutionary junta ever lasted more than 3 months…so we shall see. It's hard to predict what will happen because there are so many variables. However, in spite of all this, we are safe and we have just continued to carry on as usual.

Which brings me to Christmas and Sr. Sheila Marie and Sr. Kathleen coming to visit. Mother, I don't see any problem with this. If there were danger, we would definitely call you and tell them to stay home. And the same with Sr. Maria Berlec. Unless she is fearful herself, she shouldn't have trouble in the country. Now, if it would be better for me to stay on longer, I would be happy to do so!!!

Sr. Dorothy with the Salvadoran children

CHAPTER 4 – THE FINAL YEAR: LETTERS FROM 1980

The History of El Salvador's Strife

Sr. Mary Ann Flannery, SC

Amodern history of El Salvador is the story of political movements and the mobilization of what historian Charles Brockett calls "contentious groups" spawned from the volatile strife leading inexorably toward war.

Beginning in 1931, El Salvador had been ruled by military governments creating a political system largely closed to those from the center to the left of the political spectrum. Gradually, the "contentious groups" organized and protested to be heard. Street protests became very popular in the late 1950s. The country, though rich in natural resources, was becoming impoverished through landowners who shared very little of their profits with the campesinos who farmed the land for them.

Throughout the 1960s, the unrest mounted but a hopeful moment appeared with the election of José Napoleon Duarte in 1972. The American-educated Duarte personified the hopes of thousands at his election only to see his position swiftly overtaken by fraud, and given to Colonel Arturo Molina. El Salvador was raging on a fast track to revolution.

By the late 1970s, as Brockett points out, El Salvador experienced "…a level of sustained contentious activities…seldom matched anywhere in the region". The Cleveland missionaries were aware of the dangers in their midst, but they were concentrating on their work and making concerted efforts to avoid political involvement. Nonetheless, to discuss Church teaching in adult catechetical classes meant pointing out the Church's teaching on human rights and labor rights. To government officials such teaching meant subversive activities and anti-government propaganda.

In 1979, the civil war in El Salvador had reached its peak and murder was a common daily experience. So was torture. Most of Dorothy's letters do not describe whatever she witnessed of these crimes, but she had seen it all. She once stopped to assist a man who had been shot in the head but was dragging his wounded wife to safety because her legs had been blown off. On her travels up the mountains, Dorothy encountered torsos and headless bodies. These examples were not included in her letters but were narrated on her tapes and corroborated in interviews with her colleagues.

In March 1980, a severe blow was dealt the hopeful people of El Salvador when their beloved Archbishop Oscar Romero was assassinated while saying Mass. Cleveland's then Bishop James A. Hickey asked the veteran members of the team to stay a while longer in El Salvador to assist the newer missionaries who had been in the country only a few months. Dorothy was thus given a second extension.

At the same time, Dorothy was neither naïve nor masochistic. If she had felt her life in danger, she would not have stayed, say those who knew her best. The missionaries often said that they were respected by the military and often gave the soldiers copies of their religious instruction class notes to show there was no propaganda in them. Dorothy, particularly, would talk with soldiers whenever possible. The prevailing feeling among the missionaries was that as long as they did their work without a political agenda and as long as they kept themselves away from situations of conflagration, they were safe.

Still the violence to which they were exposed generated a personal fear and an extreme pain for the people for whom and with whom they worked. Before long, sacristans and catechists were being murdered along with parish priests. The team had to face the question: Was their presence a danger to the people?

To help resolve the concern, Fr. Al Winters, then Director of the Diocesan Mission Office in Cleveland, visited the team to direct a process of discernment to decide who of the team members should stay, if any. Each missionary agreed to stay. As a team they would re-adjust the programs that involved the laity and focus on sacramental services, the settlement of refugees into refugee camps, and the administering of the Caritas program, an initiative in collaboration with Catholic Relief Services providing food and health services.

Beginning in February, 1980, Dorothy began speaking openly about the possibility of again extending her time in El Salvador. Her letter to her superior, Mother Bartholomew McCaffrey, alludes to the discussions with Fr. Winters and Bishop but she leaves no doubt about her feelings, "I personally would feel terrible picking up and leaving them (the new missionaries) to make it on their own." On the day of Archbishop Romero's burial, March 31, 1980, Dorothy writes of the deaths of innocent people who were trampled in the press of the crowds attending the funeral. The missionaries themselves barely escaped with their lives, according to interviews with them.

By August, Dorothy shared a little more of her feelings of mounting fear and concern, "Life here has been somewhat hard – many lives seem to be taken so unnecessarily. Please do continue to pray for us – our people continue to suffer much." This third, and final period of Dorothy's life as a missionary appears more conflicted, more aware of the possible tragedy which does, in fact, end her life. Still, there is a stalwart commitment to remain and serve the people. As the war and political murder and torture mount, so does Sr. Dorothy's fear. The simple life pattern of the early missionary has dissolved into discussions of discernment as to who should stay, who should leave. The joy-filled trips to cantons to teach and distribute food and medical supplies have become journeys, tremulous with errant gunfire and wary at the sight of soldiers at check points. The simplicity of faith and service in those early years of ortho-doxy was all but gone as Dorothy grew into a greater awareness of her faith and its demands on her life as a missionary. As Panikkar has said of orthopoesis: "(it) is the accentuation of faith as love, as a personal offering, as a decision about life, as freely assumed human freedom". The middle years, the period of Dorothy's personal orthopoesis, demonstrate exactly the slow budding of what Panikkar calls transforma-tion, the act of one's life re-working into a greater whole, where the definitive lines of God's own image becomes apparent, the period of orthopraxis.

The years, 1977-1979 of Dorothy's life approached the pinnacle of Christian fulfillment: embrace of the sacred action to which one is called, a perfection of the holy, drawing the believer seam-lessly and pure, into the presence of God, orthopraxis. This sacred action is whatever strips the believer of encumbrance. Maybe it is illness. Maybe it is emotional hurt. Maybe it is martyrdom. Whatever it is, the experience, lived in the disposition of working with God – not against Him – brings the believer into full being. This is orthopraxis says Panikkar, it is that activity which actualizes the potentiality of the human being, the most complete and final stage of the true Christian life and it took place the last year of Sr. Dorothy Kazel's life.

In early 1980, the women on the team make a visit to Nicaragua hardly any more stable a place than El Salvador. Dorothy writes a narrative of her experience in trying to return from Nicaragua to El Salvador where a special team meeting is about to take place under the direction of Cleveland's Bishop James H. Hickey. The narrative is a mix of humor and exasperation, the kind of chaos reflective of the country's political mayhem at the time. "Natalie" is Sr. Dorothy's Aunt and "Sheila" is Sr. Sheila Tobbe, OSU.

A "bouncy" letter to her parents wishes them anniversary blessings and narrates the antics of the team's pets. She does not indicate any of her frustrations to her parents.

SDG

Jan. 19, 1980

Greetings!

I got your notes and $35 for more towels for Natalie. I wish I knew which blue ones she wanted.

I was happy to hear Sheila got to you so fast with all the goodies. Did she have the pictures to show you? The ones we took with my camera really came out good—I was really impressed. The Office Book you sent is not what I was looking for—but don't worry about it-I can get along without it.

How's Dad doing? I hope to call you later in the evening—but I might not get thru. I hope all is well.

Tomorrow we're leaving for Nicaragua for a few days. We're driving to La Union and taking the ferry from there. There are 5 of us going so it will be worthwhile to have a car. We're just hoping the ferry will be running—it's "temperamental"!

We should be back the same day as Paul—on the 25th. Then Bishop Hickey and Fr. Al Winters are coming on the 31 st—so it really never is a dull moment around here.

I've got to run out to a Mass with Mario (he's taking Paul's place)—so take care of yourselves—just relax and get better.

Much Love—

PS – t'was good talking to you – am glad all is well –

Love – your daughter

The following letter is a long narrative written to her parents and her community about a trip the women missionaries had taken to Nicaragua to visit Maryknoll missionary sisters, a renown Roman Catholic order of missionaries whose headquarters are in New York. The group also wanted to see how the recently inaugurated Sandanista Government was succeeding. The missionaries were prepared to support the Sandanistas because they saw them as champions of the poor as opposed to the militaristic government they had overthrown. The names mentioned in this letter are all Cleveland and Maryknoll missionaries.

The point of the narrative is to tell the readers that a simple disappointment such as closing the ferry service from Nicaragua to Honduras and thus preventing Dorothy and her companions from getting home, can lead to extraordinary action on the part of the missionaries whose Bishop is arriving from Cleveland to visit the team. They must get to Honduras by ferry and from there to El Salvador but since four of them are stuck in Nicaragua, they decide to let two go by canoe and Dorothy and Jean will wait with their 'micro', mini-van, until they can get a working ferry.

The narration demonstrates Dorothy's tenacity and buoyancy in the face of frustrating and potentially dangerous situations.

Saturday, Jan 26, 1980

Greetings!

Here I am, sitting at ocean edge in Potosi, Nicaragua waiting for our ferry to be fixed. We came over in our Microbus and didn't have much trouble leaving Salvador.

However, something isn't working well so it's being repaired & all we can do is wait because our papers have been processed. Such fun! We sent Chris & Eliz. Back to Salvador in a little boat & Jean & I are with the bus. I hope they made it over without any trouble.

Nicaragua was good to visit – they really seem to be getting the country together. I took lots of pictures of war torn areas & am having them sent to Martha Ask her to see them sometime. This year the country's big emphasis is education so there are bulletin boards & all are emphasizing this.

The Maryknoll Sisters were really good to us – we had tours of Leon, Managua & Masaza. They even took us for a swim at some friend's beautiful house. They're (the Sisters are the ones who ran the Refugee Center during the war.

Paul should have gotten back to Salvador yesterday – will be good to see him again. The Bishop & Al are coming this week, too – hope we get back in time! Therese Mary is due to come tomorrow, also – so…we shall see. We're going to eat breakfast now – will let you know what happens later.

We got home Wednesday noon via Honduras – will tell you more later. The Bishop, etc. came in today (Thurs.) to the new airport!

Love – your daughter

OUR TRIP TO NICARAGUA — —JANUARY 20 – 30, 1980

We left La Libertad and drove to La Union to catch the ferry to Nicaragua on Sunday, January 20. We arrived in La Union at 2:30 p.m. and left on the ferry at 1:00 a.m. Monday. The ride over was beautiful—the heavens were full of stars and the milky way was close and heavy. The Southern Cross rose over us. Chris and I slept on the outside benches while the other 3 stayed down inside the Micro.

We arrived in Potosi, Nicaragua about 6:30 a.m. Monday. It took about 1-½ hours to get into the country. The "muchachos" (boys) are not as organized as they should yet be. We then drove to Chinandega and on to Leon. It was an exhilarating feeling being in Patria Libre (free country). There were signs of reconstruction everywhere. It was good to see red and black Sandinista flags and signs around. In Leon, Pat Murray, Julie Miller, Gerri Brake and Rita took very good care of us and gave us the royal war tours ending with a grand visit to the Refugee Center. On Tuesday we all drove to Managua to visit with Pattie Edminston, Peg Dillon, Jean Robertson and Julianne. Again we got a total tour of the war torn areas as well as the 1972 earthquake ruins. We also stopped at what used to be a private home of Somoza (former ruler of Guatemala) that they made into a Cultural Center. Luckily the Nicaraguan chorale was there so we were able to enjoy some beautiful singing in 5 voices or more. We also took a shopping trip to Masaya and passed thru Moning Bo which was a center of war activity. We also stopped to see the beautiful volcanoes.

On Friday at 4:00 a.m. we arose and had a scrumptious breakfast before leaving for Potosi to catch the Ferry. We arrived there at 6:30 a.m. and got all of our papers processed to leave. About 8:30 a.m. we learned that the ferry might NOT be going for a few days. What to do! Well, we decided to send Chris and Elizabeth in a dugout canoe with a motor and 15 other people over to La Union. It would be about a 5-½ hour trip. But they were our connection with the "outside world" as there was no means of communication for 80 kms. However after we sent them, we were worried, as neither of them swims—and being in one of these canoes on the open ocean does leave something to be desired. However, thanks be to God, they did make it—and got safely home by the next day.

Meanwhile Jean and I stayed with the Mikro—it became our "mobile home". We lived thru Friday, Saturday and Sunday pretty well because the promise was that we would leave the latest by Sunday night. First of all in Potosi there is no drinking water or lavs. Also, the one water-spicket (sic) they had to use to wash up with did not work after Friday. There were only two comedors (restaurants) —and one was a greasier spoon than the other. This of course forced us to a 3 times a day potty schedule. We would get up at 4:30 a.m. while it was still dark; at noon we visited a friend's outhouse; then again before we went to sleep we hit the beach. We would eat in the comedor once a day—and try to share a meal. However the truck drivers thought we didn't have enough money, so they would offer to buy us our meals. In the mornings we usually waited to hear the news of the day about the ferry. Then we would go down to the beach for our dip in the ocean and then go to the fresh water river to wash up. This is also where the people wash their clothes, their kids and themselves—along with the cows and horses. Usually in the late afternoon we would go back down to the ocean and sit on the rocks and read or write or whatever. It was good getting to know the people there—there was hardly a person you talked with that had not lost a loved one in the war. One evening we even had a rifle demonstration. Three of the muchachos working there showed us everything one needed to know about rifles. The littlest one also carried the heaviest rifle! He was 18—and had been in training for two years. It truly was a war won by "tots".

The truck drivers were also an interesting group—when they know you're a religious they all want to talk about God—so that we did. We even talked about forming catechists out of some of them. Most of them were Salvadorans who drove the huge cargo trailers. They were dependent on the ferry also because they had Salvadoran license plates—and with those you can not cross thru Honduras because we are still at "war" with them since 1981)

Now Sunday we thought would be our last day there because they kept telling us it would leave that evening. So Jean and I took our last river bath (in which we used her $20 bar of Estee Lauder soap!) and put on our clean clothes. Well, Sunday night came and went—and they were promising Monday. Well then they started saying it might be another 15 days because the motor was really bad…Well then they said NO, Tuesday morning it would leave. So we hung on till about 11:00 a.m. on Tuesday—then they again started saying Tuesday night. We kept thinking we've GOT to get back—the Bishop of Cleveland will be in Salvador on Thursday—and we'll still be in Potosi. So we decided to chance going thru Honduras. The worst that could happen is that we would have to return. So we had to reprocess our papers and get back into Nicaraguara so that we could leave another way.

We passed thru the Nicaraguan frontera border without any trouble. As I pulled in to the Honduran fronters and got out of the car to go to Immigration with our passports, the man said he could do nothing for us because of the Salvadoran plates. So I talked to the jefe (boss) there who told me I had to go to Chuluteca to get permission from the Commandante to pass thru. I asked if he could be called—they said they had no means of communication. I asked if they were sure he would be there—they said yes; if not him, one of the others could do it. I asked—how do I get there? They said—take a taxi. I asked—how much does it cost? They said—$25. I said—who's going to pay for that—I don't have that much money! So I finally got a man in a pick up truck to take me in for $10. We first went to one cuartel (barracks or department)=and then got sent to another. They told me the man I needed to see went to Tegucigalpa and NOBODY else could help me. Then they said he should be in by 5:30 p.m. (this was 3:30 p.m.). Meanwhile my truck driver friend had to leave—so there I sat waiting. At 20 to 6 they proceed to tell me that he most probably wasn't coming back because it was late. I was not too happy at this point.

They told me to come back the next morning. I left VERY upset looking for a taxi in a city where I had never been. I then ran into 3 civilians and exasperatedly asked them where I could get a taxi—so they told me to wait right there and then asked what was the matter? So I told them my plight. And they encouraged me and said I certainly should be able to get help before going back. So they told the taxi driver my plight and he took me to the personal home of Captain Aguilares. He, of course, was NOT home but his son said he just left so he should be some where near. Well, we went looking around for him and couldn't find him. So, we went to another Captain's house—but he hadn't come home yet. So we returned to the first place. This time his wife and second son came out to talk to me to hear my plight. So the son went with us to find him.

After looking in every park, restaurant and bar in town, we finally found him in front of a delicatessen drinking a Pepsi with two buddies. So he came back to the house in the taxi with us. After listening to my story he proceeds to tell me there is NOTHING he can do for me. He instead, sent me to the head of Transito. This man was bien amable. When I walked in he said, what could I do for you? I said—Help me! I've got to get back home—and I told him my plight. He kept holding his head and assuring me that he would think of something. So he says—I can't help you but I know who can. So he sent me with one of his blue and white uniformed men BACK to the place where I had been sitting originally. This is now about 6:50 p.m. Around 7:00 in walks some Captain. All the soldiers there stood up and saluted and the guy at the desk told him my whole story without pausing for a breath. He then went to his office for a while. When he came back out he sent one soldier to buy vitamin pills for his little girl. Then he proceeds to call his wife and chitchat with her. Meanwhile

I'm beginning to get a bit upset, thinking this is the man I'm supposed to talk with. Well, luckily, it was not! About 7:15 the soldier at the desk tells me to go inside to talk to the Commandant (Head of the Army in Culuteca).

Well, it was like a movie. I walk into this huge warehouse size office room with air-conditioning. There was a huge desk in the middle with this enormous gentleman with cigarette holder and cigarette behind it. Behind him is this very red drape. To his left was a huge map of Central America. To his right was a drawing board. To the right center was his television. I could hardly believe it. He, too, was bien amable. And asked—what can I do for you? I said— I've GOT to get home! My problem is that I have a car with Salvador license plates. Well he then reiterated all the laws that tell I can't pass thru Honduras. I said—But I've GOT to! Then I told him our whole Potosi story and how the ferry wasn't working and we didn't have water, etc. So he had one of his "peons" working there give me a big glass of ice-cold water and he started making the necessary phone calls, etc. Well, he finally got me cleared thru and gave me a note to take to some Colonel. Before leaving he said, do come back again—but when you don't have such problems. He was really dear—I was so grateful to finally get the O.K. to pass thru. So my taxi driver and I finally got back to the frontera about 9:15 p.m.

Meanwhile Jean had been babysitting the Mikro. Neither of us had been signed into the country—but here we were. Before I even got back, the jefe who made me go to Choluteca assured her that I would get permission. This was because he had received the info from the Conmmandante. Because it was too late to pass thru, we spent another night in our Mikro. The next morning we had to take the front plate off- and because we couldn't get the back one off they just covered it with paper and tape. Then we had to have a soldier go with us to the other boarder. Two others came along to get dropped off at other places. At the other Honduran border they were waiting for us and processed us thru as quickly as possible. Then we had to put on the front plate and uncovered the back plate and passed into the Salvadoran frontera. This was quite a treat for them because cars with Salvador plates NEVER pass thru Honduras. So they asked—how did you do it? I said—with GREAT difficulty! But we made it—thank God! Our 4-day trip to Nicaragua cost us 6 days to get home!

"Persistence On The Tennis Courts And On The Nicaraguan Border: My thoughts about Sr. Dorothy's Life and Mine".

Dorothy Chapon Kazel

The following essay was written after I was stranded in a Rochester, New York hotel because of a snowstorm several years after Dorothy's death. I share it here because it emphasizes the persevering spirit Dorothy exhibited in the above narrative of her experience in Nicaragua.

Life at our house is always a spontaneous combustion of people, ideas, and opportunities which combine to fill the air with sparks of laughter and groans of surprise at the constant need for change and adaptation to make Mom's new ideas work. Dorothy arrived on the scene on her home visit in August an opportunity to mix fun, friends, and action. I wondered whether my friend Mary Ann with her deep sense of commitment to spiritually energized projects would like to meet my sister-in-law, Dorothy, "the missionary from El Salvador." I thought Mary Ann and I might even have the chance to introduce her to a game of tennis. A day on the tennis courts, what a contrast to the greens of El Salvador. I chuckled as the idea caught my fancy and grew stronger.

A call to Mary Ann brought her to our home in no time. With the telephone ringing, with the children popping in and out and the dog close behind, Mary Ann quizzed Dorothy, over fresh cups of coffee, probing her with deep questions: "What is our mission in life?" "How can I connect my life in suburbia with the issues raised by American involvement throughout the Third World?"

To the tennis courts, I thought. A battlefield where we could really hit a few ideas back and forth. I placed a quick call to our local racquet club. Court time was available. This was terrific. My son Danny and I, Mary Ann and her son Patrick would be able to concentrate seriously on our competition, after I had lined up Dorothy with the ball machine on court 6. Aha! My missionary sister-in-law was about to exchange her sandals for sneakers and her bible for a tennis racquet.

Dressed in a rare assembly of assorted tennis clothes and gripping a borrowed racquet, Dorothy began her basic instructions in the game of the pros. From "shaking hands with the racquet" to "meeting the ball," I coached her with all the details of professional techniques. Confidently, Danny and I faced our opponents and left Dorothy with the friendly one-armed bandit, the ball-machine. We left Dorothy practicing her shots. The mother-son competition began. The stakes were high: lunch for the winners! Our opponents were in top form: acing their serves, dropping shots, using cross-court volleys and executing superb net plays. The Kazel's returned with strong forehands, double back-hands, good lobs and a lot of top spins on ground strokes. War was declared on the court. As the third set began, the score was tied. Patrick urges his mom on cautioning her to "watch her alley," while Danny told me to "poach on the next shot." Concentrate. Match point.

Ka-boom! Balls seemed to fall from the heavens onto our court. We turned to see a ball machine gone wild and our swinging "tennis-nun" laughing at the haphazard array of tennis balls, dancing and tumbling unto her court. Competition had been interrupted by comedy. We joined in the laughter, enjoying her first experience with tennis as much as she could.

Undauntable! That was my sister-in-law. This was a characteristic which would carry her through many situations.

Being a missionary was not an easy life as she mentioned in her letters living in a canton only to eat beans and tortillas, enduring the heat and mosquitoes, fighting malaria and dysentery. In the letter to the family she described an experience which had comical overtones despite the military scenery with its interactions as documented in the foregoing letters. On the weekend of January 20, 1980 Dorothy, Jean, Sister Chris Rody, and Sister Elizabeth Kochik had left La Union for a short visit with Maryknoll friends in Nicaragua. The ferry boat from Salvador left at 1:00 A.M. Dorothy and Chris slept outside the white van while the others slept within it. In her letter of January 26, 1980 Dorothy remarked about her trip to Nicaragua saying; "The ride over was beautiful. The heavens were full of stars and the Milky Way was close and heavy. The southern cross rose over us."

Dorothy described the run-around of that trip in a way that reminded me of the time she was on the tennis court, hitting those wild tennis balls.

Given the political complexities among the countries of El Salvador, Honduras and Nicaragua, our Dorothy persevered doggedly to get from Nicaragua, through Honduras by land back to Salvador. For me, this experience illustrated how deeply the military there was woven to the daily decisions of life. Particularly, I contrast my sister-in-law's joyful bewilderment at the tennis court's machinery with her ability to work with the military's respect for order and rules, arriving at successful compromise.

According to Dorothy in her letter," the southern cross of the first night had shone protectively over the little white minibus and those who had used it as home." This same little minibus would be found, burned on a Salvadoran roadway about one year later on December 3, 1980.

As I sit typing these contrasts in the life of my dear friend, and sister-in-law, is it by chance that I too have been stranded but in Rochester, New York, on a cold winter's night, five years from Dorothy's own January experience? Is it because of one of the worst cold blasts in recent years, an Alberta Clipper that I have had the time to write these words about a "southern cross" in a Salvadoran night sky? As I type these words, I look out my hotel window to see a lighted cross from a nearby church in this cold winter, night sky.

The following letter is one of the last letters to her parents. It is an upbeat and simple record of an ordinary day. It is obvious that Dorothy has chosen not tell her parents anything of the death and torture she witnesses daily. "Jo" is Jo Spicuzza an advocate for orphans in El Salvador, who lived in Cleveland. She died tragically in a house fire several years after the letter was written.

May 19, 1980

Greetings!

First of all I want to say – HAPPY BIRTHDAY! AND HAPPY ANNIVERSARY!

Want you to know you're thought about and prayed for on time! I've been living in the Port lately and haven't had a chance to get any cards – so – I'm afraid this will have to do.

Thanks so much for the clock you sent with Jo - it looks great in the kitchen. Also the film is appreciated. You are so good to do all that.

Did you get the checks and money from Jo O.K.? I'm sorry I didn't write you a note then but it was a RUSH job. She really is some gal. She's so good to do all this. The kids she's bringing back are really cute. There's lots of paper work involved in getting them out. She' had her troubles with that.

Chris is here at the Port with me again tonight. Jean isn't back yet – maybe next week. She's in Guatemala studying. Her puppy dog continues to grow – rapidly! The kitty is getting big, too. For the last couple mornings she's come on to my bed about 6:00 am with a MOUSE in her mouth! Such fun! Her newest thing is going up in to the roof thru this little hole she found. Our ENTERTAINING animals.

Other than that, life goes on. I'm taking my First Communion Teachers swimming this Saturday – should be fun.

Anyway, do take care of yourselves and enjoy the SPECIAL days. Chris will be in Cleveland around June 11 – so you'll probably see her some time. Hopefully we will crossover so we can have a goose and gander party together!

Much love — your daughter

The following is from Fr. Dave Fallon who wrote this for the Cleveland diocesan newspaper. Attached was a note from Dorothy to her superior and an indi-

cation of the growing concern she had for the people of El Salvador.

June, 1980

Dear Friends Back Home:

On Sunday morning after Liturgy, I was preparing for Baptisms as usual. I quickly looked over the records to see if everyone was present. One young mother was there with only the godparents, so I asked if the father was coming. "No, Father, he left me," was all she said. Nothing more needed to be said, I have heard it so often that I almost expect it. "He left me" are words that, for me, point out part of the sad plight of so many Salvadoran families without fathers.

So many couples live together without the sacramental support of marriage; so many children grow up without fathers in the home. It is one of the symptoms of the physical and spiritual poverty, and it tends to be repeated through the generations. It also clarifies our persistent efforts to encourage marriage commitments. It is an uphill struggle. Generations of poverty, the cultural obstacles to marriage especially in rural areas, and the lack of true understanding of sacramental commitments are hard to overcome.

However, there is a readiness in the people to respond to the Gospel message. Often, after one of the weeklong mission programs, a number of couple come forward desiring to share in the sacramental life. We thank God for this visible progress in our pastoral work, which is surely a sign of the grace at work in our faith-filled brothers in Christ.

Naturally we continue to be worried about the turmoil and violence in El Salvador. Yet we are convinced that the Gospel message plays an integral part in the struggle for justice and peace, and we are proud to represent the Cleveland Diocese In its faith outreach to the long-suffering people of El Salvador.

Several of the team are away for a few weeks of study and we look forward to their return. All of us are in good health and spirits and send Christ's peace to all of you.

God's Blessing!
Fr. Dave Fallon and the
Cleveland Latin American
Mission Team

Dear Mother,

Thank you so much for the $20 I found in the letter you sent- that certainly was a surprise. I also got my appointment and the list of the others – thanks so much.

Sr. Christine will be in Cleveland by June 11 for her sister's vow day. Fr. Paul and John will also be in – they're taking that priest course at the seminary. Hopefully, I will be in by July 14 – if not sooner. I will still be taking the 2-week courses at Maryknoll – July 27- August 9. Hopefully, I will also get a chance to sit in on some chapter meetings. A lot seems to be happening this summer.

Life here has been somewhat hard – many lives seem to be taken so unnecessarily. Please do continue to pray for us – our people continue to suffer much.

I will be praying on June 16 – we'll see if the Holy Spirit wants to make you work for another 4 years. I wouldn't be surprised – you've been so good. Thanks so much for your giving in so many ways.

Please keep us in your prayers - Much love -

S Dorothy

As the unrest in El Salvador escalates, Dorothy still found time to address family events and concerns. The following letter mentions Carla Piette, MM, who drowned while taking some people across the shallow part of a river. A storm began to rage before they could get to the other side and Carla, along with Ita Ford, MM, were carried away with the swelling river. Carla pushed Ita to safety on a tree stump, but could not cling to it herself. Ita survived only to be killed with Dorothy a few months later.

In these first letters, Dorothy mentions family events and concerns, trying to keep the focus away from her and the mounting horrors surrounding her.

It was obvious through Sister Dorothy's words that violence was escalating through the entire country of El Salvador.

August 31, 1980

Greetings! *(To Jim and Dorothy, brother and sister-in-law.)*

Are you people still running off to colleges every weekend?? I hope that "back –to-school" work is almost over for you. It WAS fun going down to Florida with all of you – thanks for making it a fun trip. I can imagine Colleen is getting to know her way around Tampa quite well by now.

Well, we've been doing quite a bit of running around since I got back. The Maryknoll Sisters are still around. They came from New York, Chile, Panama, Nicaragua and Guatemala for Carla's funeral that really was a tragedy. Her body was carried 15 kilometers down the river. The miracle was that Ita survived. She was carried 1 kilometer down the river and then luckily came upon a tree trunk. After much time she got herself out of the water. They didn't find her till 6:30 the next morning. She was badly bruised and has bronchitis but is better now. What an ordeal. It's still all so hard to believe.

Anyway – that's what I've been doing – a lot of running around to the hospital etc. We're meeting tomorrow morning to get ourselves organized. Actually, I still haven't gotten all my goodies put away that I brought down – such fun!

Pray for us – Much love –

Aunt Dorothy

The following was written to Mother Bartholomew, General Superior of the Cleveland Ursulines. It is much more graphic and unsettling in their description of the danger surrounding the missionaries and their people. "Sr. Regis" is the Major Superior of

the Vincention Sisters who visited Vincentions Sr.
Elizabeth Kochek and Sr. Christine Rhody on the
mission team.

Sunday, September 7, 1980

Greetings!

How did the Community Day go yesterday? I
hope all went well.

Jean is going on vacation on Tuesday so I thought
I would take advantage of the situation and send you
a letter which will be mailed by Jean Donovan who
was arriving for a home visit from Florida so I can
tell you what's happening. If you have talked with Fr.
Al Winters or Sr. Regis you probably already know.

First of all, there was a tragic accident with one
of the Maryknoll sisters – Carla.

She drowned in the river on the way back from
a village after taking a man who had been a prisoner
back to his family. So we've had various Maryknoll
sisters with us until this point. The other sister who
was with her – Ita – survived after being carried down
the river a kilometer. She's doing o.k. Although the
full impact has not yet hit her.

Here at the parish level, things are down to
a minimum. The one thing we do have going is
Confirmation preparation. Other than that, we are
at low-key because of this, Mons. Uriosti and Fr.
Fabian have asked us to help out in other way. Since
there are mostly "refugees" who have had to flee
their home, there are now 7 refugee centers in San
Salvador. Christine is managing one of them. She's
there Monday –Friday and then comes to Zaragoza

102

on the weekends. Jean and I will be helping the Maryknoll Ita, when needed. She does have another sister living with her but they have a transportation problem. Ken is opening his Casa Communal as a Refugee Center for children – those who are lost or orphaned. We hope to call it a Hogan del Ninos so it doesn't attract too much attention. Details are still in process. Anyway, that's to give you some idea of what's happening.

The situation here is still diabolical. The killings are continuing. I managed to come across 3 cadavers on the road Friday and then went into one of our villages to find out they killed the father of one of our girl catechists. Zaragoza also has been hit by the "death squad". You really wonder how much more these people can suffer.

I want to finish this to send out. We were at a "Refugee Center" meeting this afternoon - one big problem as always is money. There are refugees in 9 places and keeping them supplied with food and fire-wood is a problem. If you know anyone who would like to donate, please have them send us the money thru the Mission Office - we would appreciate it.

As you probably realize, we can't write or talk about these things out in the open – that's why I thought I'd take advantage of Jean's trip. John Loya will be in Cleveland some time after Sept. 15 so you will probably here more from him. Also Paul Schindler will be up the end of October or so – so you will continue to receive some news.

Please do keep us in your prayers – we will do likewise. Do give my love to all!

God love you –

Love – S Dorothy

These two letters are to Sr. Martha Owen, OSU and Mother Bartholomew respectively. They touch on the ugliness and reality of the deaths of catechists and simple people: an old man, a young girl clutching a song sheet, a group of middle-aged men most likely husbands and fathers. "John" is missionary John Loya from Cleveland. "Jim Kenney" is the new missionary priest from Cleveland; "Jamie" is the nickname for Fr. Jim McCreight, now in Cleveland. The other persons are from the parish.

September 15, 1980

Hi Cutie!

John Loya is leaving for the states today so I thought I'd send these "recuesdos" up. I don't know if Cindy etc, got one either. Give them to those who want them – I thought Sheila T, Michael and Rose might want one, too.

Alls as well as can be. Jean left Tuesday – Jim Kenney came in – is in Chirilogua till John gets back – then he'll come to Zarogoza. Please tell Jaime I'm trying to locate Bernardino – they burned their house in Conchagua so we're not sure if he is in the capital somewhere or out of the country. Joaquin Serrano was here yesterday. He certainly is "maturing" – was wanting to know about everyone – said there's been lots of trouble in La Union. They even propped up 3 cadavers on a bench in the park facing the church. A catechist in Playas Negras is supposedly dead also. Life continues to be a little absurd—to know what today will bring.

> Gots to go – take care—Hello to all –
> Love ya — D

Tuesday, September 23, 1980

Hi there!

I think the Maryknoll priest superior is going back to the states tomorrow, so I wrote a letter to Jimmy Carter and I thought I'd write one quickie to you, too—so you know you're right up there at the top.

Life here gets more grueling all the time. I think the actual war may be in October or November. Yesterday, there was an enfrentamiento in the cantons above San Jose V.N.-after they searched various houses there in the pueblo at 1:00 in the morning. It seems that several truckloads of soldiers with all their communication equipment etc. (this is what I wrote to Carter about) was in Santa Maria around 6:00 a.m. and killed 10 people from there and Palomar. Supposedly there are 10-15 more people dead in Palomar and Lotes. I went up with Rosa Lidia yesterday and saw the first 10 but when it began pouring rain we had to leave so I didn't get to the other places. However, one was an old man coming down the road with 3 cows—another was a young kid going to wash at the well—another was a 12 year-old-girl who had the words of the song about Ernesto Barrera in her hands—the others were men mostly in their late 30's to mid 50's. Practically all the jovenes are gone out of that area—so they just killed the fathers of the family—really disgusting.

I might have also told you that on September 15 four men attempted to kill a bus driver in the Port. The police killed and captured two-and one got away. Today in the paper from Tamanique there was an article about Tamanique saying they have a list of 800 subversives from there and they knew where all the arms are, so…I guess we just wait for another enfrentamientl Anyway, that's all the "cheery" news for now.

Chris is doing great in the refugee center—she's using all her creative and domestic skills, which is good. We've been at more meetings regarding refugees-and there's always a million complications. Ken still hasn't gotten but two kids-so we shall see. I said something about this at the meeting today because one of the centers said 30 kids were coming to them today and they already have over 100 or so. Jean is in Ireland; John Loya should be in Cleveland now. Paul is coming up Oct. 27-maybe you'll see him-he's bringing Edi (Roberto's sister). Oh, Fr. John Murphy (diocesan representative from Cleveland) is coming to visit tomorrow-twill be interesting to see him again. I still don't even know where to begin to find out. I'll have to talk to Joaquin Alvarez again. Joaquin Serrano sends his love-he was here the other day. Don't be surprised if he lands on your doorstep one day!

Do take care-and do pray-we need it desperately at this point. You just wonder how it's all going to end...

The letter, referred to above, which Dorothy sent to President Jimmy Carter follows.

Tuesday, September 23, 1980

Dear Mr. President:

My name is Dorothy Kazel and I am a North American missionary working in the Central American country of El Salvador. I have been here for six years and have seen the oppression of the people grow worse every year.

My reason for writing this letter comes from an experience I had yesterday afternoon. I realize my experience is a very COMMON happening here, but it's one that truly makes a person sick. And it makes a North American even sicker because of the help our country has given to the Government here — as it was stated — for "vehicles and communication."

Early Monday morning (September 22, 1980), the Army soldiers of El Salvador make house searches in San Jose Villa Nueva. This in itself is a terrorizing tactic when at one o'clock in the morning when everyone is sleeping, soldiers with rifles and equipment come pounding at your door. Of course, if you do not open the door, they will knock it down. You then have to present your papers proving who you are, etc.

It seems that this group (of soldiers) kept going further up the isolated road to the cantons above in their HIGH POWERED TRUCKS and their COMMUNICATION equipment.

About 6-6:30 in the morning, they killed 10 or more people in one cantone and then went farther up (the road) and killed another 10 or more people. One old man was coming down the road and three cows-he got killed. One young man was going to wash down by the well—he got killed. One young girl about 12 years old had in her hands the words of a song which had been written in honor of one of the priests who had been martyred. They (the soldiers) claimed she was a subversive and killed her.

There were three masked men with the soldiers pointing out the houses to them and naming the people in them. When taking a man from his house, the soldiers never asked him if he was the "name" they were looking for. When a wife asked, "Where are you taking them?"—There was no answer. No words of explanation were ever given.

Now I realize these soldiers are looking for "subversives" and they may have a right to do that— but do they have a right to do it in this manner? Do they realize how many really INNOCENT people they kill because they have received wrong infor- mation? Do they investigate the information they receive before they come and kill people?

And the most appalling thing to me is that I am a North American and MY government gave them money for the "durable equipment" they have so that it's relatively easy to get into the worst cantons without much trouble and kill innocent people because of the wrong information they have received.

I REALLY WOULD LIKE TO KNOW WHAT YOU THINK OF THIS SITUATION, Mr. President and whether you really realize how many innocent people we are helping to kill. How do you reconcile all of this?

Sincerely,
Sister Dorothy Kazel

To her brother Jim and his wife, Sr. Dorothy gives only the slightest hint of the challenges she faces. But her subtle second to the last paragraph speaks volumes.

Sunday, September 28, 1980

Greetings!

Guess what! Your Christmas present should be coming! I found this article in PSYCHOLOGY TODAY magazine –an advertising gimmick. They're sending you a pair of Diamond earrings (each diamond of the pair is a genuine .25 pt. 10 – facet round diamond and will be accompanied by a Certificate of Authenticity to that effect. It's coming from Abernathy and Closther – so let me know if you get them!

Anyway – that should be fun – I hope you get them ok – and that they're nice!

You asked about my "illness" – there's nothing to worry about - I had amoebic parasites and have taken the medicine for them – hopefully they're gone. I didn't even know I had them – there was no "discomfort – so – it's a common ailment one can pick up down here.

Life here continues to be the same as ever – They say October will be bad - whatever that means. We shall soon find out. Just KEEP praying

We've been having lots of rain – as a matter of fact our yard is quite flooded right now – but it's good. We usually get tremors after the rainy season.

Dorothy

DIAMONDS ARE FOREVER
Dorothy Chapon Kazel

The following is an essay I wrote upon learning that Dorothy was sending me the diamond earrings she referred to in the above letter. I still have this special gift though they are imitation diamonds. When I wear them, I feel her close to me.

Diamonds are forever and so are my feelings for Sister Dorothy, my sister-in-law. She was a true diamond, shimmering with warmth, sparkling with life, breathing with hope.

One of my fondest memories was corresponding with Sister Dorothy. Her letters were like gems popping up in my mail box at the most unexpected times. Her last note came in November, 1980 asking me to keep an eye on my mail. "Guess what?" she wrote. "Your Christmas present should be coming! I found this article in PSYCHOLOGY TODAY magazine – an advertising gimmick. They're sending you a pair of Diamond earrings (Each diamond of the pair is a genuine .25 pt. 10-facet round diamond and will be accompanied by a Certificate of Authenticity to that effect.) It's coming from Abernathy & Closther – so let me know if you get them! Anyway – that should be fun – I hope you get them okay – and that they're nice!"

Nice, I thought – that's an understatement.

Diamonds! My heart jumped every time the mail came. It wasn't the size or value of the diamond. I knew Sister couldn't afford the Hope Diamond and I was relieved when I later learned that the earrings cost only $5.00 a pair. It was her thoughtfulness, her love that brought me joy.

Rereading her letter, I chuckled. Thoughts of Sister and her diamond gift, heading toward me, highlighted my day. My mind wondered over diamonds and the special sentiment they convey. To young people, it's the first burst of love, to married couples, it's the specialness of caring; and to Sister and me, it was the beauty of our enduring friendship.

Suddenly my mind focused on the work and dedication that goes into the making of a diamond. It's much like the making of a friendship.

A diamond is known by its color, clarity, and weight. The best diamond is colorless because it acts as a prism allowing light to p ass effortlessly through it and consequently, it is transferred into rainbows of color. Our friendship was like a prism of light. And, like a diamond, it would last forever.

Fr. Schindler's Team letter to the Cleveland Catholic paper informs the diocese of the activities of each of the missionaries during the time of war.

September, 1980

Dear Friends,

I would like to begin this month by thanking all of you who have responded to the martyr deaths of Armando Arevalo, the sacristan of La Libertad, and Carlos Gonzalez Jerez, the young man I was raising in La Libertad, with so many prayers and condolences. At a time like this, one really feels the bond we have with the universal church and especially the strength we have as an extension of the church of Cleveland.

As we continue to work we see a steady strengthening of faith in the lives of so many of our people. Here is La Libertad many of our activities have been modified and new expressions of apostolate have risen to meet the needs of the times. With so many people having to flee from the war – zones of the country – we find Sister Christine Rody, Jean Donovan, and Sister Dorothy Kazel working with transportation to and organization of refugee centers. Fr. Ken Meyers has been housing in the casa communal of Zaragoza – children who have been separated from their families. The Archdiocese along with Catholic Relief has been coordinating these efforts but there is still always need for continued support and prayers.

In His love, Fr. Paul Schindler
and the Cleveland Mission Team

Dorothy writes her last letter for the Cleveland Diocese one month before her death. She mentions events in the letter which she did not live to see. Is it premonition or a strong sense of solidarity with those who have died, including Archbishop Romero, which inspires the line, "The steadfast faith and courage our leaders have to continue preaching the Word of the Lord even though it may mean 'laying down your life' for your fellow man..."

November, 1980

Cleveland Latin American Mission

Dear Folks Back Home,

December is almost upon us. Time surely is moving by quickly – and at times one wonders just WHERE it is going!

What does December bring for us here in El Salvador? Let's take a look. First of all, it will bring us the Advent season – a time of waiting, a time of hoping, a time of yearning. Yet in the midst of this we will also be in celebration as the feast of the Immaculate Conception is the patronal feast in the Port of La Libertad and the feast of our Lady of Guadalupe is the patronal feast in Chirilagua. When celebrating the feast in the Port, we try to include everyone so on the First Friday in December we have a Mass for the Anointing of the Sick. This means that we take our jeep, pick-up and minibus and go up and down the hillsides picking up the sick and bringing them to the celebration in the church. It is something they appreciate and look forward to. On Sunday, December 7, we will have another special celebration – a Mass for group Marriages. Some may just be beginning married life but the majority are those who have been living together for years and are now ready to reconcile themselves with the Lord. This way they are able to do it without "fuss and fanfare" and spending money unnecessarily.

All of this goes on as normally and ordinarily as possible. And yet if we look at this little country of El Salvador as a whole, we find that it is all going on in a country that is writhing in pain – a country that is waiting, hoping and yearning for peace. The steadfast faith and courage our leaders have to continue preaching the Word of the Lord even though it may mean 'laying down your life' for your fellow man in the very REAL sense is always a point of admiration and a most vivid realization that JESUS is HERE with us. Yes, we have a sense of waiting, hoping, and yearning for a complete realization of the Kingdom, and yet we know it will come because we can celebrate HIM here right now!

We would like to once again THANK YOU (as we are still in the Thanksgiving season) for your continued support of us here in El Salvador and we ask you to please continue praying for us and the people here. They are the Lord's "little people" struggling to survive – to make it alive through another day – and needing His daily loving help to do it.

Thank you again.

> In His Peace,
> Sister Dorothy and the Members
> of the
> Cleveland Latin American
> Mission Team

Dorothy is thinking of plans for returning to the States after the first of the year. She continues to mention the need for quiet and reflection which the Maryknoll Center in New York may provide. This is her last letter to her friend, Sr. Martha Owen.

November 5, 1980

Hi Cutie!

Your Halloween card was great – THANKS! We all enjoyed it! Did I tell you we went to Simans on October 28 with the Maryknollers and Franciscans – plus Chirilagua? Then we had a "dress-up" party in the night. John Daily and Ron Potter came too – so it was a nice time. It's our ESCAPE from reality!

I think Chris already wrote you about Paz's son – Mario – dying. Jim Kenny and I were out there for the Mass last Wednesday. They all still miss you – I told them t'was mutual. We also went to a house Mass in Tapiagua – arriba de Cimassoa. The people there all remember you and asked about you and send Saludos. So you see, you are still very present here!

Have you seen Pablo (Fr. Paul Schlinder) yet? Hope you don't mind all the work I sent. I've been taking care of the last group of people I brought down – not like Chris – I go 2-3 days a week to see how things are, etc. I've got my fingers into too many other things to give a permanent commitment there. They are dear...!

We've been planning trips home. I'm not sure when I'll leave yet – maybe by mid-March. I'd still like to get to Bolivia if possible – and then spend a few quiet weeks at the Maryknolls cloister in New

Mexico. We shall see. Chris is all set – except now she's talking about going to Bolivia with me if we went in January – TO KNOW what we will really do!

Do take care – Sure hope all is ok with you. I don't know any more about Marta Gloria cuz I haven't seen her. Love you lots – D

In response to Sr. Dorothy's letter to the President of the United States, Dorothy received a reply from John D. Blacken, Director, Office of Central American Affairs, which stated:

November 7, 1980

Sister Dorothy Kazel
Parroquia Immaculada Concepcion
Puerto de la Libertad
El Salvador, C.A.

Dear Sister Kazel:

I am responding to your letter of September 23 to President Carter concerning our policy in El Salvador.

We deplore the violence in El Salvador which is continuing at a high level. We have made clear to the Salvadoran Government our hope and expectation that it bring the violence under control from whatever source, right or left, official or unofficial. As you undoubtedly know, it is being carried out by both extremes.

However, the leftist opposition has refused both the government's offer of amnesty announced

October 15 and the Conference of Bishops' offer to mediate announced October 18. The FMLN has announced what it terms as the "final offensive." In such situations involving widespread violence from a variety of sources it is tragic that innocent people become the victims. Nevertheless, the government's plans for elections and reforms are moving forward and may succeed in alleviating some of the conditions which have spawned the violence.

Sincerely,

John D. Blacken
Director, Office of Central
American Affairs

The last letter written by Sr. Dorothy Kazel was to her niece, Cheryl Kazel. Twirp was the missionarys' cat.

Parroquia Inmaculada Concepion
Puerto De La Libertad
El Salvador, C.A.

November 21, 1980

Hi Cheryl –

You're getting this AFTER David and Colleen because I didn't have your address. It's just a little something I thought you might enjoy having for your room. You're also getting TWIRP'S paw prints as she just walked across the paper!

I hope this finds you well and enjoying school once again. Your mom says you may be changing to Michigan next year. Would this mean you're changing y our major also or do they have the same course there?

Well, Cutie, take care of yourself and enjoy the holidays for me. Can't believe I'll be home next year at this time – probably freezing to death!

Love –
Aunt Dorothy

REFLECTIVE ESSAYS ON SR. DOROTHY KAZEL FROM THOSE WHO KNEW HER

Remember Dorothy Kazel, OSU
Sr. Martha Owens, OSU

When Dorothy and I were young nuns-in-training we would escape into the Motherhouse fields picking wild berries. One such adventure gave Dorothy a colossal case of poison ivy. I spent some time at her bedside, doing what I could to break the monotony of her confinement. In our berry picking and her recuperation, I began to know of her deep faith and of her vision of what it meant for her to be a woman of faith, an Alleluia from head to foot.

Miss Bony-knees, we called her, when her physical ability outstripped our puny efforts at basketball, softball or water keep-away. Now Dorothy wasn't the greatest player, but she would try anything and endure everything to make her dreams come alive. Thus when she called to have us sisters play basketball with a group of teenagers at Sacred Heart Academy, she knew we'd be there. Somehow she knew that we could truly bring the love of God to her students through our pathetic efforts at basketball.

That same spirit was active when we lived in one moldy room during hurricane Fifi, studying Spanish in Costa Rica. To and from class we would pass children with whom Dorothy would strike up a conversation even though we knew only a few words of Spanish. Half in English and half in Spanish, Dorothy would fearlessly carry on a conversation while two and sometimes three children were attached to her swinging hands. Her facial expressions made them laugh as she hunted for simple nouns, not even daring to try the more challenging verbs. The exchange was heart-to-heart and far more eloquent than polished speech. It seemed she was saying "I love you and so does God".

Dorothy always wanted things to be better, especially for the poor. Surely, you could imagine her thinking; a better diet for the poor would help. And thus Dorothy managed the Caritas Food Distribution Program. Her commitment wasn't just about pulling strings and jumping through the red tape of a society obsessed with intermediaries. But when the food finally came, she was there on the distribution lines picking up 50 pounds sacks of powdered milk or rice and moving them to the stations on her slight, bony-knee frame.

One special task Dorothy loved to do was to visit the humble hut of a young blind girl she was preparing for First Communion. For weeks, Dorothy made the arduous trip over cobble-stones, ditches, and unpaved paths to reach the dirt floor home and begin the class for the day, As you can imagine, the classes were as much friendship building as faith development. And as the special day drew near, Dorothy saw to it that a suitable white dresses with appropriate veil were a part of the blind girl's apparel. Following the first Communion celebration, pictures were taken to record the happy event. The pictures were more for Dorothy thank the blind girl. For the blind girl, the kind and gentle churchwomen's presence was captured on the film of her heart.

After the special day passed the journey was made once again down the unpaved path and over the rough cobble-stones. But this time it was by the blind girl with a gift tucked under her arm headed for the nun's house. Dorothy received her former pupil and the live chicken with great pleasure. The chicken was given in gratitude for the precious visits, the friendship and the classes. Dorothy often pointed out that the live chicken was one of the most touching gifts she had ever received.

Just as the Disciples on the road to Emmaus, we both listened to the radio broadcasts of the Sunday mass homilies celebrated by Salvador's Archbishop Romero, and our hearts did indeed burn within. When he paused in his teachings, the affirming applause of the campesino at the Cathedral mass could be heard over the radio. Dorothy would interject the same sentiment as felt by the campesino but Americanized to the chant of "go get'em Bishop!" She loved his retort to those who made fun of him. Once Romero responded, "The prophetic mission is the duty of God's people. So when I am told, in a mocking tone, that I think I am a prophet, I reply, 'God be praised!' You ought to be one too."

Dorothy was never intimidated when she genuinely believed that the truth was on her side. Dorothy rode her motorcycle down the mountain to the hacienda in her region and spoke with the duenos, the rich landowners, about Archbishop Romero and his concern for the dignity of every human being. He articulated the vision she held in her heart of life someday being better for the simple campesino. The duenos told her that the Archbishop had betrayed them because he said to them "Stop the repression." And "We want to be the voice of those who have no voice." He said this because he knew that the only voice the campesino had out of fear for their lives, was when their applause was heard over the radio during his Sunday mass.

During a Team Retreat in Salvador on a warm, sunlit afternoon, after having lived and worked together for five years, Dorothy and I went for a walk to decide who should stay in El Salvador and whose time would be up. Since the stakes were so high and neither of us wanted to leave, the emotions ran deep. Yet as we walked together along the dusty paths, it was easy to be honest with Dorothy because she was honest with me. After each of us presented our thoughts, it became clear to me that I should be the one to leave. It was a time of great joy for her and great sadness for me. I sent her to tell the team and left to be alone with my life changing decision. That decision also became life changing for Dorothy in another way.

After informing the Team of our intentions, Dorothy found me and stayed with me to ease the consequences of my decision. Much work together remained to be done before my departure.

Leaving Salvador was difficult but not impossible. The constant harassment of being stopped by the guardia to search us, the tapped phone lines, riding as body guards with the native priests, or the news of yet another kidnapping or priest being killed or atrocity, left us concerned and careful. Thus, leaving the surreal situation and traveling home together the roundabout way through Canada, was a diversion for Dorothy and I. On the train up the West Coast of California, as we passed the city where her former fiancée lived, I learned more of her feelings toward the young man to whom she had been engaged. There was tenderness in how she spoke of him.

Dorothy was soon back working in Salvador and in a tape recording to her I was bemoaning my returned status and complained to her about the ridiculous, unnecessary task of cleaning out the "clean" cupboards at the convent. I remembered our work in Salvador – taking dying, dehydrated babies to the hospital, giving food to families who would cook it over a wood fire while standing barefoot on a dirt floor, finding a coffin for a young catechist who died in the mountains while picking coffee beans, or being stopped and harassed by the security forces at gun point. Dorothy replied in a letter that if it was any consolation, she and Jean had also just cleaned out the cockroach-infested cupboards of the La Libertad parish kitchen. Her comments helped me survive reentry.

As I wrestled with my reentry to convent life, Dorothy and I kept up a constant stream of communications. By letter or tape or phone call she let me know of the situation in the country, what was happening in my villages, on the team and to my friends. Three months after I left, a special letter arrived from her that spoke of what I should do in case something happened to her or the team. I read it thinking that the precaution was a good idea that would never be needed. I saved the letter with all the other communications.

For those of us who knew Dorothy, she was made of the same stuff as the rest of us. She was a human being and in her humanness she struggled to know God's will for her. For someone who was always one step ahead of others when it came to knowing what was on the agenda next, it was surprising to experience her in those final days searching for what God wanted of her. Her constant refrain became "To know" mimicking the Spanish "saber?" –who knows? Her inability to see a future was, if you will, an omen of what was to come.

A few days before her premature and violent death I called to wish her a Happy Thanksgiving. She sounded so weary and distraught about the escalating violence in the country. Knowing her as I did I fully believed she acted on what she felt was right and just. She gave up the chocolates she loved as a personal petition to God so that the repression in the country would stop. She asked our superior to extend her time on the mission so that she could accompany the people in spite of the existence of very real dangers after the death of Archbishop Romero. I believe she offered herself to God to be used in any way God would want so as to relieve the suffering of the Salvadoran people. As her brutalized body and those of the other churchwomen were pulled from the shallow roadside grave in front of the camera lens of the news media, the horror of the Salvador experience and the suffering of the Salvadoran people became the personal horror of the world.

Upon my return to St. Malachi convent after having been at the Kazel's home since word came that Dorothy was missing, I went immediately to my treasure chest of letters and tapes to find the one I knew I had to reread. Her request to "please explain it for me" became a mandate. And even though I felt as Jeremiah the prophet who complained to God "I know not how to speak" there was no Dorothy to complain to and say to her, not me, choose another. Thus I had to let the words of God to Jeremiah be my guide, "The Lord extended his hand and touched my mouth, saying, See, I place my words in your mouth!" (Jeremiah 1:6, 10).

MEMORIAL REFLECTION

Sr. Mary Rathbun, OSU

In many ways Dorothy Kazel was an ordinary woman who did ordinary things in an extra ordinary way.

Although I, too, was with Dorothy in our formation years here at the motherhouse, I really got to know her and her sense of commitment and dedication when we were both assigned to teach at Ursuline Sacred Heart Academy located in East Cleveland from 1965 until 1972.

Dorothy taught business, typing and shorthand in what was called the portable. Her students loved her because she really cared for each of them individually. She would spend hours listening to their problems before and after school. In the fall and spring, Dorothy could be seen on the front steps of the white portable building listening to one or more of her students. In the winter the heat didn't always make it to that building so Dorothy would often be seen inside the building with her shawl (which we wore as a coat in those days) and her gloves while she was teaching.

Dorothy was very faithful to her personal and community prayer; she would go to chapel before supper and often afterwards. Her relationship with God led her to always want to do more for others and to give of herself for others.

In addition to her teaching business in high school, Dorothy learned sign language and taught catechism to the deaf and later taught typing at the Martin Deporres Center in Cleveland on Saturdays and evenings.

In 1967 when I returned from a summer of study in Arizona, Dorothy asked me if I had seen any American Indians. I told her that the Papago Indians lived on a reservation in Tucson, and the next summer she went to teach the Papago Indians on that reservation.

While still teaching at Ursuline Sacred Heart Academy, in order to do even more for her students, Dorothy began working on her masters in counseling at John Carroll University in the evenings, on Saturdays and during the summer. At that time she had not made any plans to go to El Salvador even though our first Ursuline Missionaries to El Salvador left Cleveland in 1968.

During this time in East Cleveland, the various churches held many ecumenical services and Dorothy participated in as many as she could. The Thanksgiving services at the Methodist Church across the street from the school and the ecumenical retreat that she and I attended were very influential in broadening her vision of church. It was at this ecumenical retreat when Dorothy was asked what she would like on her tombstone that she said: "I want to be known as an Alleluia from head to toe." I thought at the time how appropriate that saying was for her.

Dorothy was always joyful and very generous. Since I was responsible for directing the plays, I would always ask her to help me with the business part. She would organize the students to ask for advertisements and she would run off the programs on the hectograph machine. We could see the light on in her classroom late at night while she was working on the programs; then she would return to the convent with black ink splattered on the white parts of her habit from the hectograph machine. Dorothy would also collect the money for the advertisements and tickets.

I remember the year our convent was robbed; it was during the time of the play production. When Dorothy heard that the robber had gone into our bedrooms and taken what he could find, she ran to her room to check on the money from the play. Soon she came out of her room laughing, saying that she didn't think he would find the money in her girdle box and he didn't.

Living in a community of women can be a type of white martyrdom at times, but Dorothy enjoyed being with her sisters. In fact when she had to go to the hospital for minor surgery, she insisted on being brought home so she wouldn't miss the Christmas party we were having. That evening during the party, Dorothy began to hemorrhage so an ambulance was called; the ambulance driver said he had never seen such a skinny Santa as Sister Kathleen Burke in a red suit and beard.

After struggling to keep Ursuline Sacred Heart Academy open by introducing experiential learning and going door to door in the neighborhood to develop awareness of our presence in the area, it became clear that the school could no longer stay open. After the diocese announced the closing of Ursuline Sacred

Heart Academy, Dorothy and some of the rest of us moved in 1972 to Beaumont School for girls (as it was called then) in Cleveland Heights. Since only a few of our students from Ursuline Sacred Heart continued their education at Beaumont School, most of them went to Villa Angela Academy, we began to minister to a completely different group of students. Typical of Dorothy, she jumped right in, teaching typing and doing her internship in counseling. She was liked immediately by the students and became their confidant as she had been to her students in East Cleveland.

It was after she knew Ursuline Sacred Heart was closing that she told us she had applied to go to El Salvador and that she would be leaving Beaumont in 1974 to prepare to replace the first two sisters who were ministering there. When Dorothy left, she told me to "take care of my girls"—the students she still kept in contact with from Sacred Heart and the ones she knew at Beaumont School.

There is so much more that I could say about the inspiration Dorothy was and is for me personally and for all with whom she came in contact. As a woman dedicated to God and to her Ursuline Congregation, she used all her gifts, skills and abilities for the glory of God alone. Dorothy loved God and showed it every day so that her short forty-one years were enough for her to be away from her beloved. Whether or not Dorothy is ever canonized as a saint of the church, we who knew her are sure that she is a saint and that she is still with us through her generous and joyous spirit.

CELEBRATING THE LIFE AND MINISTRY OF SR. DOROTHY KAZEL, OSU NO HAY TEMOR EN EL AMOR, LOVE CAST OUT FEAR

Sr. Kathleen Cooney, OSU, PHD, LSW

I remember seeing Dorothy on the front steps of our motherhouse, the afternoon we entered, September 8, 1960. As one of 20 young women, "dressed in black from head to toe" with a black cape and skirt, a white collar and cuffs and black "nun's shoes," Dorothy was one of us, -ready to enter into the process of becoming an Ursuline Sister.

In this swirl of our families, her sunny blond head and contagious smile were eye catching. Although Dorothy was a few years older because of her experience teaching in the St. John College's Cadet Program, she fit right in with those of us who were 17 or 18 years old, fresh from high school, part-time jobs and summer fun. Soon after the Entrance ceremony and meeting our Novice Mistresses, Mother Kenan and Mother James Frances (Sister Anna Margaret) we were quickly were brought into the convent schedule: waking at 5:20 am, getting to morning meditation, learning how to do our novitiate charges, attending classes, learning to say the Office, trying to keep the various kinds of Silences and funneling our leftover energy into novitiate recreation activities: Some of which: roller-skating on the Loading Dock, or ice skating in the winter. In the summer, playing baseball, planning picnics and feast day celebrations with their plays and parodies of song. Wasn't Dorothy just a bubbly, energetic, fun-loving personality? Wasn't she just one of us?

The theme of martyrdom was introduced to us on the occasion of our clothing, when we received our religious habit. Father Frank Osborne spoke of white and red martyrdom. He said: "there is a red martyrdom and white martyrdom,"… "Red martyrdom is the giving of one's life for a sacred cause. White martyrdom is the daily dying to oneself." (Henaghan). Most of us assumed that the era of red martyrdom was over, and the daily dying to self would be our challenge.

On this Clothing Day, Dorothy was given the religious name of Laurentine. Once, we were joking in the hall: "What's a Laurentine?" At that moment, Mother Marie, the General Superior, came swooping around the corner and with her brown eyes blazing, told us that "Laurentine" was an Ursuline Nun martyred in the French Revolution. We were humbled and silenced at that thought. In that moment, Mother Marie told us, solemnly and prophetically that there would be days in the future of religious persecution for the church.

What was our novitiate experience like with Dorothy? The Novitiate was composed of three age groups or Sets. With the reception of the habit, we became first year novices and began or Canonical year, Dorothy did all the so called "dumb things all novices do", like putting the ham scraps on the green beans in the kelvinator rather than into the pork'n beans in the oven, and she lost a little of her hard learned religious decorum as she took after the jeep

– realizing the clutch had not held as it rolled down the hill near the Boiler Room, …She also picked branches off of Mother Marie's "Baby Pine Trees for Christmas decorations. And, I was often with her as we just made it home for the sacred "4:30 Saturday Holy Hour," after driving what Dorothy called "the ulcer gulch run" to Joe Bova's Shoe Shop. She just one of us, wasn't she? Yes, she was one of us.

While we were in the womb of the novitiate, the windows to our semi-cloistered world were opened. Pop John XXIII initiated the revolution of Vatican II. Thus, the challenges of the late sixties and early seventies opened wide the frontiers of service for religious women. The times were exciting, and challenging! Talk about paradigm shift! We were pushed into the depths of ourselves examining our vocations and outward as Sisters in the World (Suenens).

In the challenges of responding to the changes brought forth by Vatican II, Dorothy was someone you just wanted to be with and be an Ursuline. After our professional formation as students at Ursuline College, we were missioned to teach. Dorothy went to teach business course at Ursuline Sacred Heart Academy where I joined her later. Together, we taught the Sophomore Service – Beatitudes in Action Program – and worked with the other Sisters there to create innovative learning experiences in the local community. And – we all had fun – especially with Miss Sever and the Sacred Heart Gym Leaders on their overnight weekends at Camp Cheerful and with Sister Ann Winters and various student retreats.

She was one of us. She was active, flexible, and involved. She searched for ways to address social problems as they came to her in everyday life and she looked beyond her everyday life experience for the something more, the something more to give and to be. I would catch a glimpse of her contemplative side, when I would come upon her sitting in Sacred Heart's small chapel gazing at the tabernacle, or be surprised by a window sill full of modge-podged rocks with quotations on them which she had been working on. Nature, for her, was an awesome experience. And a source of joy. She carried a suitcase full of rocks from Arizona back to her Mom on the bus. The depth she possessed was rarely shared in a very public way. Although, I remember finding ourselves at a few charismatic prayer meetings, professing our love of Jesus in the song and even answering an Altar Call.

Although I was not aware at the time we entered in September, that she had just broken her engagement to be married in July, I have come to see her decision as the root of her martyrdom. Because it was such a fundamental choice to love Jesus Christ it was one that impelled her to search, question and continue to ask: What do you want of me, Lord? In the days before December 2, 1980 she wondered: "What else" can I do for the people of El Salvador? The song. Pescador de Hombres, sung on the day of her burial in the foyer outside this chapel by the Mission Team Members answered the question for me: "Lord, you have come to the seashore neither searching for the rich nor the wise, desiring only that

I should follow… O Lord, with your eyes set upon me, gently smiling, you have spoken my name; All I longer for I have found by the water, at your side, I will seek other shores."

Motivated to seek the cutting edge of service in the Church, I think she took her direction from the powerful words of Archbishop Romero. In December of 1977, he said: "To be a Christian in this hour means to have the courage that the Holy Spirit gives in the sacrament of confirmation become for us a sacrament of martyrdom." (Romero, 17) I think she found the answer to her quest for complete union with Jesus in El Salvador.

So when in August of 1980, she said to me: "We are the Church." I knew she was going back, as she looked at me from a chair in the Grace Residence Hall. I, like Peter telling Jesus he must not go to Jerusalem, had wondered to her: "Do you think your going back might endanger other near you?" Her simple, direct answer summed up her mission and vocation, her life's choices: "We are the Church." It would mean being with the people in their suffering, being in the jaws of death and military violence and being Jesus, as well as offering food, shelter and refuge in their own country. In a country where some bishops wore the uniform of a military Colonel, she, Jean, Maura and Ita aligned themselves with Archbishop Romero and shared, as he did, the same fate as the poor.

So, how has the woman, this sparkling, talented woman of deep faith challenged me to live? How has this friend who exhausted herself in the last days before she was killed, deepened my spirit? The life and death, of my friend, Dorothy has connected me with many of the people with whom she shared her life. In her actions, I consider the following:

- Don't underestimate the value and importance of the ordinary in one's life.
- Distribute Caritas rice and beans to refugees,… or find a way to feed the hungry.
- Pick up Terry Alexander and Mattie Dorsey at the airport and then go back and get Maura and Ita …or give someone a lift, extend yourself.
- Write a letter home that immortalizes the struggles of El Salvador's people, or just write a letter.
- Comfort a mother whose son has been killed by the death squads, or just comfort someone.

Dorothy's winsome ways were born of reflection, thought and prayer. Many little decisions and factors in her life brought together a woman who could be decisive and assume responsibility in a crisis, and yet be fun, creative and even a little silly to cheer her companions in the realities of life.

Does she not challenge us to say with her: "We are the Church."? Does she not challenge us to be "Jesus …here with us now."?

References:

Henaghan, Father John, S.C. *White Martyrdom: The Story of Father Damien.* "There is a red martyrdom and white martyrdom", an Irish monk wrote on his parchment scroll one. 'Red martyrdom is the giving of one's life for a sacred cause. White martyrdom is the daily dying to oneself.' Damien smote himself day by day." As given to Sister Kathleen Cooney by Therese Osborne after the funeral liturgy of Sister Julianne McCauley's brother Christopher (Fall 2005) and at Ursuline College when Therese visited Sister Anna Margaret Gilbride before returned to El Salvador.

Romero, Oscar. (1988) *The Violence of Love.* Trans. & Ed. By James R. Brockman, S.J. CA: San Francisco. Harper and Row. 17.

"HOW SHE CAME TO KNOW THE POOR: A REFLECTION ON THE LIFE OF SR. DOROTHY KAZEL, OSU"

Sr. Mary Ann Flannery, SC

She was born June 30, 1939 in Cleveland, Ohio as the world was convulsing furiously in the throes of a war not soon-to-be-ended. Her father, Joseph, was a buyer for Standard Products, a producer of solvents, her mother, Malvina, a secretary for W.S. Tyler, a manufacturer of wire and mesh products. Malvina also tended the family home in a Lithuanian neighborhood where neat yards and perfectly appointed frame houses gleaming with white paint and colorful awnings stood welcoming and alert, festooned by tree lawns with gallant maples.

Nearby was the butcher shop, the grocery, the drug store, the hardware, any store you might need just to get the family through the minor crises of daily life. For bigger items, more expensive tastes or seasonal shopping, you hailed a streetcar and headed downtown only a mere seven miles away to Higbees, or Mays, or Sterling-Linder Davis, the giants of retail and fashionable clothing.

But the proprietors of the neighborhood shops knew all their customers by name. They attended the same church, sent their children to the same schools. During hard times a family need only hand a note to the store owner and he would furrow his brow, out of sympathy, not distrust, and the need was quietly supplied. No questions asked. Pay when you can.

Within ear-shot of the street a child could measure the time of day by what she heard. When she walked to school in the morning a bellicose whistle from the yawning furnaces of steel factories into which hard-working men would descend, all but swallowed the fresh awakening of the day. Raw life had gathered its momentum.

In her classroom at St. George's Elementary School, the petite and sunny Dorothy Kazel would squirm into her seat having skipped down an aisle of shredded paraffin wax which the nuns distributed on classroom floors to gather the dirt and dust from the streets. With her classmates, Dorothy would learn reading, writing, arithmetic, geography—and so much more. Here she watched her friends stare out the windows stained with the grime of the furnaces mixed with the slushy fallout of Cleveland's winter skies thinking momentarily, of their fathers some-where deep in the bowels of those furnaces hoisting long, burning shovels of molten iron to be made into parts for ships and tanks. She thought she was very fortunate because her father did not work in the furnaces.

Walking home from school at three o'clock in the afternoon, a child's attention is drawn to another diurdian reminder as the factory whistle wafts across Cleveland's leaden skies. Shift change. End of the day for many workers now emerging from the hellish hallows of what they called, 'work'.

Dorothy skips into her yard and up the rear wooden steps of her house to the kitchen door and announces perkily as she opens the door, "I'm home."

She smells dinner cooking because her mother always arrives home early enough to start it and then takes on chores like ironing curtains, polishing the living room furniture or sewing Dorothy's new skirt or dress in the sewing room. Dorothy throws her books on the dining room table and heads for the telephone to call girlfriends she had just talked to in school. There are plans to be made.

After all, she has to arrange, with her best friend, the details for Saturday's roller skating party at Skateland Arena on Euclid Avenue. The list of invitations is growing and Dorothy couldn't be happier. "The more, the merrier," she tells her friend. She has become part of Skateland's Roller Skating Team and Malvina has paid for skating lessons in which Dorothy will learn to twirl the baton while performing the cuts and circles of footwork on skates. She absolutely loves skating. The sequined blouse with full arms and the plaited tutu are every girl skater's dream. Malvina has added little jewels to catch the spotlight when, of course, it focuses on Dorothy as she dances away on her roller skates. Dorothy's excitement mounts because if she practices enough, she might perform in front of critical audiences when she is in high school, only a year or two away.

High school. More freedom than now. And boys. Malvina and Joe are already talking about an all-girls Catholic high school and Dorothy chafes at the idea hoping they will forget by next year when she has to enroll somewhere. But they don't. And Dorothy has no immediate plans for a career, just a gnawing attraction to help people whatever that means. It's a flimsy attraction she thinks. It floats in and out of her mind, just enough to give pause. It really doesn't take hold. Not yet.

Right now the skating party is all-important. When the day of the party arrives, Dorothy hosts a pajama soiree so everyone can 'crash' at her house after the excitement and energy of the roller rink event. Dorothy and friends take over the second floor of the family home. Bags of potato chips are washed down with favorite soft drinks. Malvina has baked brownies but insists that everyone eat a salad first, a salad from a bowl as big as Joe's backyard vegetable garden. Around the bowl everyone giggles sitting on the floor laughing about teachers and boys. Somewhere in the reverie a friend says she won't be attending Notre Dame High School because her parents can't afford it. The others tell her she's lucky and they laugh away her embarrassment and what might be her greatest wish. But Dorothy turns her eyes away and stares blankly at the salad and the brownies in a universe of chatter. She senses, once again, her good fortune.

Dorothy Kazel has all the advantages of a middle class childhood. Joe and Malvina are first generation Americans imbued with the hard work ethic and absolutely committed to the goals they have encouraged Dorothy and her brother, Jim, to achieve. Jim is two years older than Dorothy. He is handsome and shy but give him a saxophone and some delightfully wild spirit rips out of him and he belts the horn from side-to-side, up and down, his face a bulging red moon flushed with song and concentration, his eyes tightly shut under furrowed brows. Jim is in his element dreaming of a career in music, maybe with a dance band, as Dorothy spins about dancing to his music in the living room.

In high school Dorothy meets the Notre Dame Sisters for the first time. She is quietly intrigued by them and watches them over the next four years trying to discover why such talented women would settle for a life of teaching and some kind of spiritual commitment that seemed interplanetary at best, far out of reach for her, the fun-loving, spirited teenager whose practical goal at this point was to study in the commercial program and become a secretary, like her mother.

After all, a secretary's career could put one in touch with men who led businesses and maybe this would generate a marriage of promise. But as high school continues, the only problem, the only fly-in-the-ointment of this arrangement is the heavy substance and challenge of religion class. And, of course, as time goes on, the annual retreat.

When one tries to muffle the incense of inspiration, religion class will unravel it and make it unavoidable. The teachings of Jesus packaged in the encyclicals on human justice along with a growing awareness that teachers provide in the stories of Dorothy Day and Charles de Foucault begin to make sense. Reading about and discussing these people, these resources, carrying their mystery to class retreats and stealing quiet moments just to think on them draws the attention of classmates. They wonder

at Dorothy's periodic thoughtfulness. Social awareness is slowly tightening its hold on her heart.

It's no surprise that Dorothy applies to St. John
College, a women's college in Cleveland and near
her Euclid, Ohio home. By now, the Kazel family
has moved to Euclid hoping to expand the possi-
bilities of the American dream in a suburban atmo-
sphere where their two children can maximize their
educational opportunities. Dorothy majors in education, not business as expected. St. John College is a
college of education and nursing primarily for religious sisters but attractive to lay women for its cadet
program in teaching. The program was designed
to prepare teachers for fulltime jobs after only two
years of college with a guarantee to finish their
degree requirements at a considerable discount while
teaching in a Catholic school.

In this setting, Dorothy once again observes the
spirituality yet ordinariness of her religious classmates. It is probably from an Ursuline classmate that
she learns of a job opening at one of the schools they
staff, St. Robert Bellarmine. Something inside of her
stirs a growing awareness of the needs of others and
she sees a barometer of sorts saying that the more
education one has the more one succeeds in life.
Education, then, becomes the means, the way she
will help others. She decides on a career in elementary education.

With all its fun, all its tangled web of intellectual
preparedness and social activities, college becomes
a deepening source of challenge under a nascent
spiritual rigging climbing alongside the studies of

the secular, but somewhere inside she is beginning to make sense that there is a connection between teaching and spirituality, between commitment of helping others and placing one's life on the altar of self-abnegation. She's not sure it's for her, this entrance into a life of dedication that she sees in the women religious around her.

The key is not being sure.

When you're not sure, an idea lingers sometimes invading your life, an errant messenger knocking on all the doors of the soul demanding to be investigated, to be resolved. But, in some cases, like this one, it is a Voice. You really cannot annihilate such a Voice.

After two years of college, Dorothy is hired to teach third grade at St. Robert School, and begins her lifelong friendship with the Ursuline sisters. The children are full of life and Catholicity; but the young teacher thinks there's more. The Voice tells her this.

To augment her teaching salary, Dorothy takes a job at Bailey's department store in Cleveland, especially during holidays and seasonal vacations. She works in the cosmetic department and loves fussing over makeup and jewelry. One day, a young man is walking through the store with his friends. He is visiting from California and as would be expected, he teases the sales clerks as he saunters past the counters. He catches sight of Dorothy laughing with the other clerks, her hair bouncing with a yellow sheen caught under the lights, and he stops.

Over the next year Dorothy Kazel and Don Kollenborn date and a romantic relationship develops.

He proposes. Dorothy accepts. But the Voice gets stronger. Marriage and a family would not reconcile a Voice asking for a different kind of commitment, a commitment to those who have little in life. The poor? Yes, the poor. Not even teaching at St. Roberts will satisfy this Voice.

In fairness to Don, Dorothy makes a retreat which forces her to reach deep down inside with wrenching agony, inside where the Voice seems to be, the Voice she cannot quiet no matter how hard she tries. After all, she's doing all the right things: She earned a college degree, she is working a career, and she is engaged. This is what Joe and Malvina have always wanted for their daughter. But the Ursuline sisters whom she has come to know and respect while teaching with them, stand for something more. She finds their sense of commitment and their dedication to teaching an appealing goal away from a life centered on the personal happiness of making a family. The Voice is restless.

After the retreat, she realizes that entering the Ursulines is the first step to reconciling the Voice. And so, in the back of St. Robert church, Dorothy and Don sit in the shadows. She finds it nearly impossible to look him in the eye as she tightened the grip on his hand. She can't explain it but she must try it she says and he pretends to understand. She breaks into tears thanking him for everything, especially for the affirmation of being loved by such a special person. Only the occasional spark crackling from a votive candle can be heard and then the muffled sobs against his shoulder. For the next several months,

Don will stay in touch but never interfere while still hoping Dorothy will change her mind. He has converted to Catholicism, surely a sign of his eagerness to share the same faith throughout a marriage he hopes to secure. Still, he never invades Dorothy's pursuit of a religious vocation with selfish demands or envious revenge. The next summer, Dorothy will travel to California to visit an aunt and uncle and meet with Don to return the engagement ring. But, on this night, this late summer evening in St. Robert church, Dorothy Kazel's first love walks slowly into memory.

According to those who were in the novitiate with her, Dorothy was funny and mischievous but she took her spirituality seriously something one observes in the voluminous retreat notes she began making and which she continues all through her religious life. Between 1961 and 1962, the young novice writes extensively on love. "Don't suffer contagiously," she journals in the summer of 1961, "Each apostle had a big heart! (LOVE)—the capacity to LOVE. Love is the highest motive. Love makes light. Things are not hard when you are in love. Follow Him more closely. Acts of love are always found in deed rather than in what you say." In one reflection she says, "Consuming love includes totality...assuming responsibilities—LOVE." In another, "With God's grace, I desire only to LOVE Him...Love does not claim rights: no selfish aims. The general aim of love is to truly become aware of Christ dwelling in others."

In 1963 she wrote, "What is an Ursuline? A woman in love!" For the next decade of her life, despite immense popularity and success as a high school teacher, Dorothy prays, "Change my selfish heart into a totally loving heart. Melt me Lord. I am stone. I cannot give in this capacity. I am filled with self." At one point she comes across St. Augustine's famous line, "A Christian should be an 'alleluia' from head to foot." "That's it, "she exclaimed. "That's going to be my epitaph!"

During these years Dorothy still struggles with the Voice. She learns sign language thinking that ministry to the deaf might be unselfish work on behalf of people often overlooked. She becomes active in diocesan interracial and ecumenical committees. She is seeking and giving along the way. In 1969 she begins a summer ministry of teaching the Papago Indians near Tucson, Arizona, sponsored by the Cleveland Diocesan Mission Office. All of these experiences enrich her high school teaching but, still, the Voice encourages more. She is happy and fulfilled in her work but she knows, deep inside, just as she did when a teen-ager, that there is something more to be done.

Her excellent qualities as a teacher prompted her superiors to refrain from allowing her fulltime work as a missionary. As early as 1967, she writes to her superior, "I am presently 28 years old and consider myself as mature as I could be at this time…My two points that I am trying to get across are 1) that I have a sincere love for and desire to help people and for some reason, the Spanish and Indian people have a special appeal for me.; 2) I believe that catechetical work is an important part of religious life — someday religious life should revolve more closely around it." This is the first indication of Dorothy's direction toward full inclusion with the poor. But she was denied her request. Still, she listens to the Voice in her heart. She does not give up.

Finally, in 1974, Dorothy Kazel, O.S.U. is given permission to study and prepare for service in the Cleveland Diocesan Mission to El Salvador in Central America. Her excitement overflows into a note in her retreat diary of June, 1974: "Jesus I am fighting for you again. I am fighting dying to myself. I am fighting myself on my own will. Jesus, I am sick at the pit of my stomach. Give me the peace to know I am doing your Will." Dorothy has found the Voice. She now enters the happiest years of her life, for only too short a time.

In El Salvador, Sr. Dorothy Kazel is as popular and effective as she was teaching in Cleveland's Sacred Heart and Beaumont High Schools. She runs a Caritas program teaching women how to use food donations from the U.S. and other countries. She teaches children their religion and directs youth groups in social service. She takes communion to the sick sometimes in remote mountainous areas requiring horseback or the motorcycle for transportation.

As the civil war in El Salvador rages in the 1980s, Sr. Dorothy and her colleagues are overworked with care for refugees, transporting them, setting them up in camps, desperately trying to allay their fears while they themselves endure sleepless nights as bullets pierce the night air around their little convent. Before the war, Dorothy's summer vacations included workshops and classes in Latin American Church Documents which came out of the Medellin Conference of Latin American Bishops in 1968. She reads comprehensively everything she can on liberation theology and feminist theology in an effort to understand better the people she serves. Her reading leads her to a wider world of the marginalized. The Voice, it seems to her, is subdued; she is content, though fearful of what lies ahead for her. She requests an extension of her time in El Salvador because of the worsening conditions and the arrival of a new recruit for the team who will need experienced companionship. Her superiors and the Bishop of Cleveland grant the request.

In the meantime, a very real possibility of death here in the impoverished and politically abused land looms on the horizon. Archbishop Oscar Romero, the Bishop of the Salvadoran diocese where Dorothy and the missionaries work, is assassinated. She deepens her commitment to the people, and as a fellow missioner recounted, she spent hours before the Blessed Sacrament in the parish church. She refers to a "resurrection experience" in a letter to friend only months before her death following the drowning of a Maryknoll sister who was trying to save others in a flash flood. She considers the possible consequences of staying in El Salvador, but it has been a dream of hers since entering the Ursulines and stemming from the simple childhood of a God-centered life.

The once distant horizon of eternal life is closing in without her full knowledge, only her suspicion, and the assurance that when one works for the poor, one moves slowly but surely toward self-immolation, the loss of oneself in the resurrection of the poor. In a moment of pathos and under a dull ceiling light bulb in her small bedroom, Sister Dorothy Kazel writes her last letter home to be published in the Cleveland diocesan newspaper one month before her death. It is portentous of the tragedy looming unknown to her but gathering strength with each day.

"All this war goes on normally and ordinarily as possible. And yet if we look at this little country of El Salvador as a whole we find that it is all going on in a country writhing in pain…The steadfast faith and courage of our leaders have to continue preaching the Word of God even though it may mean 'laying down your life' for your fellow man in the REAL sense is always a point of admiration and a most vivid realization that JESUS is here with us."

Five days later Sr. Dorothy Kazel, O.S.U., Sr. Ita Ford, M, M., Sr. Maura Clarke, M,M., Jean Donovan laid down their lives, execution style, on a lonely hillside in San Vicente, El Salvador. Acting under orders from their superiors, five Salvadoran soldiers kidnapped the women as they road from the airport toward the Cleveland Mission. Dorothy and Jean had picked up the two Maryknoll sisters to visit the mission to determine if they would leave Nicaragua and come to work in El Salvador. In the hours following the kidnapping, the soldiers drove the minivan they had seized with their victims in it up a long hill out of sight of the local villagers drinking and terrorizing the frightened women as they drove. Several hours later, a farmer who lived near the scene of the crime heard screams and gunfire followed by the ravenous engine of the minivan and the slamming of its doors as the laughing men began the trip back to their camp. Then silence. The next day he searched to see what may have happened and came up upon the bodies of the four women buried in a shallow grave.

Many ask how Dorothy could have requested an extension of service knowing how volatile and treacherous life was at the time in El Salvador. I believe it came from a lifetime of awareness of the needs of others, an awareness that could not be silenced, no matter how hard she tried to submerge it. An awareness that became a Voice, God's Voice within her. From her childhood, protected and comfortable as it was, to her young adulthood considering marriage, to her early ministries as an Ursuline nun, Dorothy Kazel knew she was challenged to be with the poor, not just to teach them or to encourage them, or to protect them, but to stand with them and to raise her hands in their defense, to live with them—in their poverty, not hers. To mix her blood with theirs in the soil of their land. She would die the way many of her poor friends had died: tortured, raped, and shot to death while on her knees no doubt pleading for her life as she prayed for mercy. She came to know the poor by experiencing them in the streets of Cleveland, in the hearts of troubled students at Sacred Heart High School, on the reservation in Arizona, in the cantons in El Salvador. She came to know them by listening to a Voice who wanted her to be with them exclusively, even when opportunities to serve them looked dim, if not impossible. She stayed with her dream. She prayed and persevered. She joyfully ministered to them. She touched the poor. She sang with them, laughed with them, wept with them. From a slow growth of an almost imperceptible awareness of those less fortunate than her, from childhood to adulthood from missioner to martyr, finally, on December 2, 1980, on an otherwise idyllic hillside in a very poor country, and along with her very dear friends, she gave her life.

In the trial testimony the following February, one of the murderers recounted that as they, the killers, moved toward the minivan sure that the women were dead, they heard a moan and turned to see a foot move. It was Dorothy's. She was still alive. The gunman had previously misfired into her shoulder sparing her head and had not noticed it. In another moment of vicious rage, he then walked over to where she lay and fired the shot that tore into her brain in the dreadful quiet of that night. Dorothy Kazel, O.S.U. was embraced by the total Love she sought in life as she served others. And that is how she came to know the poor.

After Malvina Kazel's death (Sr. Dorothy's mother), the Kazel family found the following letter which Malvina had written to her deceased daughter some four years after the murders. Though the crime was never fully resolved, and it appeared that some

*Salvadoran military authorities had escaped pros-
ecution, the letter demonstrates a loving faith that
Malvina had looked to in order to be healed.*

Dorothy—
You didn't know what was going to happen to you.
The tragedy tore at your Dad's and Mom's heart.
We miss you very much, and hope that one day, only
known to God,
That the good Lord will grant us the privilege to be
together again in His peaceful
and better world.
We miss you very much. After four years, a healing
has come about as
a result of putting everything in the Hands of the
Lord. Or, as a result of
putting it in the hands of God.
*(Typical of Malvina, the letter was neatly typed but
unsigned.)*

**Sister Dorothy Kazel Ursuline Nuns
of Cleveland; Born – June 30, 1939;
Entrance into Ursuline Community
September 8, 1960; Religious Profession
– August 13, 1963; Gave her life in the
service of the Church and the people of El
Salvador December 2, 1980**

THE AUTHORS

Dorothy Chapon Kazel is the sister-in-law of Sr. Dorothy Kazel. An author, lecturer, and panelist who has addressed numerous professional groups. She has written feature articles for the Cleveland Plain Dealer, the Kentucky Courier Journal, and the North Carolina Catholic. She has made several television and radio show appearances. She is a wife and a mother of six grown children. Chapon Kazel published a short biography in 1986 called, THE ALLELUIA WOMAN.

Sister Mary Ann Flannery is a sister of Charity of Cincinnati is an Associate Professor of Communication at John Carroll University in Cleveland, Ohio. She was the general superior of her congregation whose sisters were serving with Dorothy in El Salvador at the time of the murders. She knew Sr. Dorothy while Dorothy was a missionary.

Breinigsville, PA USA
27 November 2010
250165BV00001B/11/P

9 781606 473214